Books by Russell Kirk

Randolph of Roanoke

St. Andrews

The Conservative Mind

Select Political Essays of Orestes Brownson (edited)

A Program for Conservatives

Academic Freedom

An Essay in Definition

by

RUSSELL KIRK

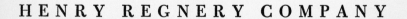

HENRY REGNERY COMPANY

Chicago   *1955*

First Printing, February, 1955
Second Printing, March, 1955

Copyright 1955 by Henry Regnery Company. Copyright under International Copyright Union. Manufactured in the United States of America. Library of Congress Catalog Card Number: 55-6452.

"Every man is not a proper champion for truth, nor fit to take up the gauntlet in the cause of verity; many, from the ignorance of these maxims, and an inconsiderate zeal unto truth, have too rashly charged the troops of error and remain as trophies unto the enemies of truth."

—Sir Thomas Browne,
Religio Medici, Part the First, VI

CONTENTS

Acknowledgment

I am much indebted to a number of scholars for their opinions and the information with which they have supplied me. I have visited a number of colleges and universities in order to improve my knowledge of the subject, and always have been received with courtesy. The general theme of this book was described by me in a public lecture at the University of the South in January, 1954.

RUSSELL KIRK

Mecosta, Michigan

ACADEMIC FREEDOM

I

Liberty and License

"ACADEMIC FREEDOM," says a distinguished editor, Mr. W. T. Couch, "is the principle designed to protect the teacher from hazards that tend to prevent him from meeting his obligations in the pursuit of truth." This is the best definition of the idea that I have come upon. And Mr. Couch goes further: "The obligations of the teacher are direct to truth, and the teacher who, in order to please anybody, suppresses important information, or says things he knows are not true, or refrains from saying things that need to be said in the interests of truth, betrays his calling and renders himself unworthy to belong in the company of teachers." I subscribe to this opinion, and I may as well state here my general convictions on the important subject of academic freedom, so that the reader may make allowance for my prejudices, if he likes.

I believe that academic freedom, an idea, has reality; and, like other ideas, its reality is more important than the ephemeral reality of particular persons and circumstances. I believe that academic freedom is a peculiar kind of freedom, and peculiarly valuable. I believe that academic freedom is *not* a hoax, but an inheritance from the wisdom and the courage of our ancestors. I believe that academic freedom is gravely threatened in our time. I believe that the causes of this peril to academic freedom are imperfectly apprehended by most

1

scholars and teachers and journalists and politicians. I believe that if we desire to preserve any institution or concept, our first necessity is to define our terms correctly, and to ascertain accurately the causes of discontent. Therefore I have written this little book, an essay in definition, hoping to assist in the endeavor to raise our discussion of academic freedom out of the pit of cant and slogan into which too many disputants have fallen in these past few years. This has not been a work wholly congenial to my cast of mind. Yet, convinced as I am that the reality of academic freedom is incalculably precious to our civilization, I have made the endeavor; and if my effort is a feeble one, I ask the reader's indulgence; for (as Newman reminds us) life is for action, and if we desire to know anything, we must make up our minds to be ignorant of much. I have done what I could, then: and I have tried to prepare myself for the undertaking by reading most of what has been written in the English language on this topic, and by conferring with people who know something of it, often by personal experience.

"Like so many of the institutional freedoms of the modern world, the roots of academic freedom lie deep in aristocratic, not to say medieval society," a sociologist of mark, Dean R. A. Nisbet, writes to me. "The university is today one of the few final enclaves that have survived (in considerable part, at least) the invasions of modern mass democracy and economism. I regard academic freedom and tenure as one of the few last and precious survivals of genuine European culture, and I am far from sanguine about our abilities to maintain it in this world of demonic fears and prejudices. If it ever dies, I think it will not be difficult to show that the pragmatic liberals with their shrill misconceptions and their worship of popular political power did a great deal to cause the death." Now I have endeavored to rise to the level of Dean Nisbet's observations on the subject, considering academic freedom in the light of recent events, it is true, but seeking to relate those

2

events to the enduring idea of a special liberty, or body of liberties, that is attached to the academic institution, the teacher, and the scholar. Because this little work is only an essay, and not a comprehensive survey, I have decided to confine my remarks for the most part to our universities and colleges, venturing only occasionally to touch upon similar questions relative to primary and secondary instruction. But the problems are almost as pressing in the schools as they are in the colleges; and the schoolteacher, indeed, commonly enjoys far less freedom of opinion and action than does the professor. If academic freedom is to be sustained and restored, probably the energy and leadership for such an accomplishment must be discovered, initially, in the colleges and universities; therefore I have directed the greater part of my attention to those institutions.

Let us return, momentarily, to the business of tentative definition. Academic freedom is a security against hazards to the pursuit of truth by those persons whose lives are dedicated to conserving the intellectual heritage of the ages and to extending the realm of knowledge. It is the right, or group of rights, intended to make it possible for certain persons (always very few in number, in any society, when compared with the bulk of the population) to teach truthfully and to employ their reason to the full extent of their intellectual powers. We will not find these rights guaranteed by any article of the federal or state constitutions, or described in any legislative enactment, here in America; and, with some small exceptions, throughout the civilized world these liberties are the product of custom and moral prescription, rather than of positive law. Nor do these rights have any easily ascertainable sanction of force behind them. Juridical thinkers of the school of Austin, then, scarcely can admit that academic freedom is a right at all; for in the Utilitarian view of rights, a right has reality only when it is expressly asserted by the authority of the state, or when (whether through the agency of the state or of some

3

other coherent group) it has positive force—in the final resort, *physical* force—to assert its claim. Nor is it easy to see how academic freedom can be anything more than a phrase for pragmatic thinkers, however much they may praise it; for to the pragmatist, the impulse of the present generation is everything, and what Burke called "the contract of eternal society" is nothing: in other words, rights have no origin in the laws of God or of nature, but are simply the products of social convention, to be obliterated when the experience or interest of the present generation ceases to approve them.

Academic freedom, in short, belongs to that category of rights called "natural rights", and is expressed in custom, not in statute. A great many people, nowadays, entertain a most shallow and unhistorical notion of natural right, despite the work of scholars like Professor Leo Strauss to restore a proper understanding of the concept. Natural right is not simply what Justice Holmes scoffingly called it, "a brooding omnipresence in the sky."* It is, rather, a moral system applied to jurisprudence: a body of belief in certain rights long established by custom and prescription, and found by the test of time to accord with human nature and civil social nature. Most adherents to natural-rights theory believe that the original impulse toward these moral rights came from a source more than natural and more than human, if by "natural" and "human" is meant simple utility and private interest; but the particular forms which the search after natural law has taken are the product of human experience in history, supported by the franchises of what Chesterton calls "the democracy of the dead"—that is, the considered opinions of the innumerable good and wise men who lived before our time. These are rights which rise

---

* Justice Holmes used this phrase (in the case of Southern Pacific Company *v.* Jensen, 244 US 205, 1917) to describe a concept of the common law which he opposed; but it also represents his pragmatic contempt for the whole theory of natural law, as expounded by the Roman jurisconsults, the Schoolmen, and the English common-law writers.

superior to particular governments and particular states; and if some arrogant political authority, or some presumptuous generation, ignores or tramples these rights, good men may justly obey the natural law in defiance of the ephemeral "law" that is set up in opposition to the moral traditions of the race and the historic experience of society.

Just such a right is academic freedom. Almost nowhere is academic freedom sanctioned (again in Justice Holmes' phrase) by "the articulate voice of some sovereign that can be identified." A man whose academic freedom has been infringed cannot successfully appeal to a court of law, unless, by coincidence, the violators of his freedom have happened to commit a breach of formal contract, of the same nature as a commercial contract. Nothing in the laws of our federal system, or of the several states, guarantees the enduring right of a teacher to speak the truth as he sees it, or to pursue the truth according to the light that is given him. In extreme circumstances, it is true, such a teacher might appeal to the general provisions for freedom of speech found in the federal Bill of Rights and in the state constitutions; but then he would be appealing not to *academic* freedom, but simply to the statutory freedom which is constitutionally guaranteed to all men, whatever their occupation or status. If academic freedom exists anywhere, then, it exists in the realm of natural rights and social conventions sanctioned by prescription; and if theorists deny the reality of natural law, logically they must deny the reality of academic freedom.

Far from believing that the silence of an "articulate voice of some sovereign" invalidates the idea of academic freedom, I am convinced that academic freedom is all the more real and valuable because it finds its sanction in moral belief and ancient usage. The very Decalogue, after all, is only partially and imperfectly recognized by the positive laws of modern states. Our dearest liberties and privileges are conferred upon us much more by immemorial usage and the dictates of con-

5

science than by statutory enactment. It is not positive law which enjoins a man to honor his father and his mother, although occasionally statute may endeavor to compel him to provide for their physical subsistence. Similarly academic *rights* are more important than mere formal contracts between universities and professors, although the state will enforce the latter and not the former. I do happen to believe that a brooding omnipresence superior to human frailty implants in us, here below, a desire for justice which never can find full expression in the written enactments of a mundane sovereign; but the particular forms which that search after justice gives to human institutions are determined by many centuries of human experience, so that "academic freedom" and "just due" and "freedom of choice" are supported by historic experience and the customs of a people. I take my stand, in fine, with Thomas Aquinas and Richard Hooker and Edmund Burke; I am in opposition to the opinion of Bentham that "right" is simply what the political sovereign chooses to dispense, and in opposition to the opinion of Rousseau that "right" is whatever gratifies the undisciplined craving of the individual. It is perfectly true, I think, that every right must somewhere find an ascertainable and reasonably definite sanction; but there are sanctions more enduring, and more to be honored, than the decrees of an ephemeral master or the appetites of an ephemeral generation.

The preceding remarks may seem to constitute a digression; but if I take high ground, it is because I am convinced that academic freedom will not endure in our age unless it is defended upon sound philosophical postulates. The confusion which follows hard upon a muddy notion of "right" already is evident in the current discussion of academic freedom. A number of persons—I respect the integrity and motives of some of them—are unable to distinguish between academic freedom and the general freedoms possessed, or claimed, by everyone, in the academy or out of it. Even when endeavoring to sustain academic freedom, some such people undo the idea by confounding it with "human rights" indiscriminately applied, or with "constitutional guarantees" which make no specific provision for university and teacher, or with a vague "liberty" which considers university and teacher only so many specks in a tapioca-pudding equalitarian society. John Locke observes, in his lucid way, that often the most voluble partisans of liberty are the least effectual defenders of it. Allow me to offer a few instances of what I mean. Mrs. Agnes E. Meyer informs us that "academic freedom is only one aspect of human freedom." Colonel Robert McCormick recently inquired (an inquiry, I may be allowed to observe, is more humble than a dogmatic assertion) whether academic freedom was really something different from the freedom of all men. President Briggs of Phillips University says that "*academic* freedom is not a thing apart, nor something vague, different or peculiar, but it is *intellectual* freedom, which seems . . . to embody all the freedoms we know and cherish so well." Mr. William F. Buckley, Jr., thinks that academic freedom, at least in its modern form, is something got up as a hoax to deceive the proprietors of universities and colleges: "For in the last analysis, academic freedom must mean the freedom of men and women to supervise the educational activities and aims of the schools they oversee and support."

Now I think I understand the chain of reasoning which led each of these persons to his conclusion; and, though it is improbable that any one of these persons sympathizes heartily with any other of the four, I am inclined to sympathize, in some degree, with each position. The idea of academic freedom has been enveloped in so much rodomontade, these past four or five years, that doubt of the idea's reality or identity is excusable. Professor Sidney Hook, in *Heresy, Yes; Conspiracy, No,* declares that "there is more sloppy rhetoric poured out per page about academic freedom both by those who believe that they are supporting, and those intent on criticizing it,

7

than on any other theme with the possible exception of democracy."* But for all that, I do not believe in the slogan, popular in certain quarters just now, that "liberty is not divisible." Liberty *is* divisible, unless by liberty we mean the abstract and perilous *liberté* of the Jacobins, which American and English leaders and people generally have rejected. It is in the name of that abstract liberty that crimes are committed. One of the great blessings of our political experience is that we have recognized liberty as multiple, made up of a large number of separate freedoms, varying with particular circumstances, and pertaining to particular groups and persons. There is the freedom to bear arms—under certain circumstances; there is the freedom of workingmen to organize—for certain purposes; there is the freedom of self-government—through representatives; there is the freedom of accumulating property—through lawful means. Not every man enjoys precisely the same freedoms as every other, nor should he want to. Academic freedom is not the same thing as secrecy of the ballot, or as security against the quartering of troops. And if the teacher and the scholar are constantly exhorted to throw themselves into crusades for the liberties of Indonesia, or the abolition of the poll tax, and they rally to such cries, they are going to find themselves with very little time left for teaching and scholarship. And then, in the excitement of chasing after other people's freedoms, they may find that academic freedom has ceased to be. For every right is married to an appropriate duty; and when the duty is neglected, the right shrivels.

For my part, I am convinced that academic freedom truly *is* a thing apart, different and peculiar, and that we would be foolish to confound it with the vaguer term "intellectual free-

* I rather think that Mr. Hook would include certain writings of mine under this head; but no matter; we must take the truth where we find it, and in this, as in much else, Professor Hook speaks plain truth. For my part, I am inclined to believe that Mr. Hook has done his share in pouring out sloppy rhetoric about democracy; and so has his adversary Mr. Robert Hutchins.

dom". *Intellectual* freedom is chiefly an aspiration; it can be sought after, most of the time, only by the solitary man of contemplation. *Academic* freedom is an historical reality, with ascertainable limits and prerogatives, to be preserved and extended, often enough, by intelligent co-operative action. As with the accurate definition of words, in the accurate description of concepts and institutions we pursue the historical method: we endeavor to learn what "academic freedom" has meant to past generations, and how it has developed, if we want really to employ the phrase sensibly. And if we apply the historical method to the apprehension of the idea of academic freedom, we will not come to Mr. Buckley's conclusion that it consists in freedom simply for the masters of educational institutions to enforce their opinions upon the teachers—though we may discover, at the same time, that academic freedom never has meant complete autonomy for teachers, or the licentious toleration of a bewildering congeries of private fancies.

I propose, then, to examine somewhat summarily, in the following section of this chapter, the historical signification of "academic freedom". The present, when we come to seek for truth in it, is found to be no more than a thin film—sometimes a scum—upon the deep well of the ages; and perhaps no one does more mischief than the visionary who endeavors to guide us by *a priori* assumptions about the unknowable future. It is only by reference to the past that we can obtain some grip upon the meaning of an idea disputed in modern society. *

---

* We are just now beginning to recover from the effects of the anti-historical twaddle that was popular enough in academic circles at the beginning of this century, and for a long time thereafter. As a specimen of this infatuation, we may take this outburst of Franz Boas, nearly half a century ago:

"The truly human ideals we find expressed where man is least restrained by historic tradition. . . . This condition prevails particularly among the masses of the people, much less among the segregated classes. . . . The intellectuals, who are steeped in historical tradition, and are therefore, on the whole, little able to think clearly, belong to this group. The rich, the nobility, the scientist, the artist, the

2

"Academic freedom is a specific kind of freedom," Mr. Sidney Hook writes. "It is the freedom of professionally qualified persons to inquire, discover, publish and teach the truth as they see it in their field of competence, without any control or authority except the control or authority of the rational methods by which truth is established. Insofar as it acknowledges intellectual discipline or restraint from a community, it is only from the community of qualified scholars which accepts the authority of rational inquiry." Now the trouble with this definition is that no such degree of liberty for scholars and teachers has long prevailed anywhere; Mr. Hook really is writing of his ideal, rather than describing a tradition or defining the phrase as it has acquired meaning from the experience of civilized society. Mr. Hook goes on to say that academic freedom is not an absolute, but that society finds it expedient to extend this freedom to the academy because society at large benefits from the consequences of unhampered inquiry. If, then, the academy either fails to accomplish its educational goals, or if it violates other moral values more weighty than academic freedom, the community does right to abridge academic freedom.[1] Mr. Hook, believing that such checks upon the general principle ought to be employed only very seldom, neverthe-

---

clergyman, all belong in their great mass to such segregated groups . . . in which the thought, couched in a catch phrase, is an almost elemental power, stimulating man to activity without any attempt to think out clearly what the catch phrase may mean or whether it does mean anything."

There could be no better proof than this passage that to be anti-historical is to be anti-intellectual. The consequences of such adulation of ignorance and denial of intellectual leadership have since been stamped upon the face of the world. The "truly humane ideals" of revolutionary Russia and Germany, since then, have reminded us that men who ignore the past are condemned to repeat it. No one falls a more easy prey to the catch phrase than the man who neglects the history of catch phrases.

less remarks that "the *justification* of academic freedom must lie in its fruits".

Here I begin to part company with Mr. Hook. He goes on to argue that the Academy, or university, is "a semi-public institution", a part of the community, subject in theory to the will of the community. I think he goes too far. Although rights may have a justification in their fruits, they may also have a justification in prescriptions; and although the Academy exists in part for the sake of the community, it exists also for its own sake, and more especially for the sake of private wisdom and private needs. "Its ultimate fruits are to be found not in the private, professional delight of the connoisseur of ideas, although this has merit, too, but in the public good which includes, let us hope, the multiplied private delights of others besides professors." I find in this sentence of Professor Hook's an ominous fondness for intellectual collectivism. And I believe that here Mr. Hook is unhistorical.

The first regular Academy of which we have much knowledge was the school of Plato. Now Plato's Academy did not exist in any immediate way for the benefit of the community; indeed, Plato and his pupils commonly were at odds with their community, in a political sense. The allegiance of the Academy was to something grander even than Athens: to Truth. For Truth, and in defiance of the people of Athens, Plato's master Socrates had died. Plato and his disciples were not public servants. They taught and studied for their "private, professional delight", and for the conservation and enlargement of Truth. It is true, of course, that Athens and all the civilized world benefited, in time, from their labors; but that is not the primary justification for the freedom of mind enjoyed and defended by the philosophers in the groves of the Academy. The community, indeed, often hampered them a great deal, and put the first of its great thinkers to death, and forced the second to flee to Megara and Syracuse, and compelled the third, on occasion, to take refuge in Asia. All political communities, even wisdom-loving Athens, tend to dread or despise their academies, so that to lay down the dogma of academic responsibility to the community, in Professor Hook's definition, is to run the risk of subjecting the liberties of the academy to the prejudices of the multitude, and to run the risk of subjecting the free human person to an abstract state. I do not mean to imply that philosophers have no responsibilities toward their fellow-men; indeed, the pursuit of Truth puts upon them very grave responsibilities; but they need always to remember that it is Truth they worship, not humanity, and that it is by Truth they must be judged, not Demos. If philosophers are treated as servants, even as the servants of a faceless Community, presently they will acquire the proverbial vices of servants, with few of the redeeming virtues of simple loyalty to persons.

Plato's Academy, for twenty-three centuries, has been to scholars the grand model of freedom to pursue the Truth. Although continuity of institutions is one principal evidence of prescriptive rights, it is not the only evidence. Our modern universities and colleges are not descended in a direct line, of course, from the Academy of Athens; but when, nine centuries after Plato began to teach, Justinian closed the schools of Athens, the idea of academic freedom was not extinguished. A memory may have as much power as a living thing, or more. And already the first of the great Christian universities, that of Constantinople, was nearly a century old when the end came to the Athenian philosophers. But my principal concern, just now, is this: the Academy of Athens, like the other great schools of antiquity, was not founded by the community, nor did it owe its primary allegiance to the community. It was instituted by private persons for their "private, professional delight"—or, to speak more accurately than Professor Hook does, to enable them to pursue the Truth without being servants of an evanescent community. And this idea of intellectual freedom, the freedom of the Academy, has ever since been the model for all men trained in the classical disciplines.

But modern learning owes even more to medieval institutions than it does to its classical strain; and, besides, there subsists a direct historical continuity between the medieval universities and much modern education, even in America. We ought, then, to pay close attention to academic freedom as it existed in the medieval university. Mr. Hook, no friend to the Schoolmen, nevertheless confesses that "within the framework of certain key assumptions of Christian doctrine, a considerable degree of academic freedom was enjoyed by the medieval university at a time when civil freedoms for the citizens of the community was hardly an embryonic concept."* Although Mr. Hook intends to be fair here, I think he has missed the point, which is this: there was freedom in the medieval universities *because* they existed within a framework of "certain key assumptions of Christian doctrine", not in despite of their Christian origin. Just as the Platonic Academy was free *because* its primary allegiance was to the Truth, and not to the community, so the medieval universities were free *because* their allegiance was to the Truth, as it was given to them to perceive it, and not to the community. Their framework of assumptions did not restrain them; it protected them. The Schoolmen, like the philosophers of the Academy, were dedicated men—dedicated to the service of Truth. The philosopher, in Greece, was a man apart, superior to many human frailties, especially the varieties of concupiscence; and he was revered accordingly. The Schoolman was a cleric, usually vowed to celibacy, and expected to lay aside, so far as he could, the vanities of the world; therefore he was privileged accord-

* This generalization also verges on the unhistorical: a very considerable degree of civic freedom was enjoyed by the burghers of most of the towns in which universities came to be established. But at least Professor Hook recognizes that the freedom of the universities was not *derived* from the freedom of the general community.

13

ingly. These men were not servants, but masters; not the agents of the community, but seekers after divine love and wisdom. They undertook their work with a high consecration. And the academy, or the university, was a place consecrated to the apprehension of an order more than human, and a duty more than mundane.

I propose to relate these considerations, in a little while, to Professor Hook's view of academic freedom. But just now I turn to some remarks on the same subject by Dr. Robert M. Hutchins, in his *University of Utopia:*

> The universities from which our own are descended were founded in the Middle Ages. They were either corporations of students wanting to learn, as in Italy, or of teachers wanting to teach, as in France. Corporations that had unusual legal or customary privileges for the purpose of carrying out the intentions of the incorporators were common in those days. In some Italian cities the Guelf and Ghibelline party clubs, sworn to subvert the state, were recognized corporations specially licensed to work on the project they had in view. The university corporations of the Middle Ages at the height of their power were not responsible to anybody, in the sense that they could not be brought to book by any authority.* They claimed, and succeeded in making their claim good, complete independence of all secular and religious control.
>
> In asserting and establishing this claim, they had one inestimable advantage: they had no property. If any secular or religious authority sought to control them, they would simply move away. . . . All the medieval universities that amounted to anything were of the same general type. They were formed because somebody wanted to learn or somebody wanted to teach. They maintained their independence on the ground that it was necessary to their corporate function. They did not regard themselves

* In part, this is bad history. The Guelf and Ghibelline factions, for instance, never were tolerated if their avowed intention was to overthrow the very city-state in which they existed; it was their hostility to the distant Emperor or the distant Pope which sometimes was tolerated. Some of Mr. Hutchins' generalizations on the constitution of medieval universities will not bear the scrutiny of anyone who has taken the trouble to glance through Rashdall's three volumes on the subject.

as servants of either church or state. They thought of themselves as co-ordinate with both. . . . Although the men produced by the medieval universities became leaders in the church and in the state, they did not advertise that their function was to produce such men. Such men were a by-product of the enterprise in which they were engaged, which was singularly like the enterprise of the University of Utopia: it was the discussion of the most important questions. They would have been startled if they had been asked to justify their existence in terms of the service they performed for society, for they would have had no doubt that the discussion they were carrying on was its own justification.[2]

Here we are treated to that commingling of sound sense with imprudent generalization which characterizes much of Mr. Hutchins' writing. It is true that the medieval master and student did not consider themselves servants; and, more in jest or bravado than in sober earnest, they spoke of the three powers that govern society—Sacerdotium, Regnum, Studium. In this sense, but in this sense only, were they "not responsible to anybody": that, like other medieval guilds (which ordinarily had a churchly origin, especially in the North), they governed themselves in most matters, sometimes even in the administration of criminal justice. But self-government is not the same thing as irresponsibility. Italy excepted, throughout Christendom the universities were responsible to the church, and sometimes to the state as well. Chancellor and rector, especially in the North, ordinarily were great ecclesiastics; founders and benefactors, with a few exceptions, were bishops or princes, when not popes or kings; the masters and the students were clergymen or in minor orders; and while a university ordinarily was exempt from the governance of local clergy, nevertheless it could not stand against the great prelates for any length of time. Bologna, Mr. Hutchins' favorite example, had the freest constitution of all, and, like most of the other Italian universities, is a partial exception to my remarks above; yet clerks, even there, formed a part of the student-body, and

Christian doctrine permeated all the teaching, and in time Bologna and its sister universities came under the direct supervision of the Pope and the monastic orders. All this is not to say that the medieval universities were compelled to submit regularly to the inspection and direction of the officers of the state, or of the inferior clergy; on the contrary, they taught substantially what they liked, as they liked; no one presumed to set himself up for a greater scholar than a Schoolman—that seeming a manifest absurdity in medieval times, though in this enlightened age we are encouraged to take a different view. But Mr. Hutchins is confused, and confusing, when he tries to suggest that the medieval universities acknowledged no authority spiritual or temporal. Such a condition would have been as impossible as the ideal state of academic freedom suggested by Mr. Hook, or as the regime of the University of Utopia suggested by Mr. Hutchins recently. If, as Mr. Hutchins says, the American university cannot really expect to be free of the persons who supply its funds and its students, neither did the medieval university ever really expect to sever itself completely from clergy or laity. Every such university was established by a Papal bull; most had their origin in a cathedral school or some other churchly foundation; and many had royal charters, into the bargain. Substantially, the universities were parts—though autonomous parts—of the Church. (The Church also had other parts substantially autonomous, like the great orders of regular clergy.) The Schoolmen were persons dedicated to the conviction that the fear of God is the beginning of wisdom; and their students were either candidates for holy orders or else young men learning law or medicine in an atmosphere of religious veneration.

We ought not to endeavor to revise history according to our latter-day notions of what things *ought* to have been, or upon the theory that the past is simply a reflection of the present. The medieval universities did indeed enjoy academic free-

dom, in a larger measure, probably, than any academies before or since. But they enjoyed that freedom *because of* their
status as religious institutions, not in despite of it. They did
not obtain that freedom from the "community", nor as bands
of enterprising secularists. Their prerogatives rarely were
challenged, because everyone assumed that the universities
were a natural part of the order of things here below, and because no one had presumption sufficient to sit in judgment
upon the universities. When, during and after the Reformation, the universities lost their status as so many autonomous
parts of a universal Church, they lost their independence correspondingly. In Protestant Europe, they came under the
jurisdiction of the national churches and of the rapacious national monarchies; in Catholic Europe—although to a lesser
extent—they came under the jurisdiction of the reinvigorated
and consolidated Papacy, and of the sovereigns who, as in
Spain and in France, made royal influence over the church
establishment within their realms a condition of their support for the Roman cause. In fine, the dissolution of medieval
universalism meant that learning, like nearly everything else,
was forced to submit to new and more rigid dominations. With
the complete or partial secularization of society which followed upon the French Revolutionary era, in nearly every
country except Britain the universities were stripped of what
remained of their old rights, and became little better than
state corporations.

My point is this: in the Middle Ages, as in classical times,
the academy possessed freedom unknown to other bodies and
persons because the philosopher, the scholar, and the student
were looked upon as men consecrated to the service of Truth;
and that Truth was not simply a purposeless groping after
miscellaneous information, but a wisdom to be obtained, however imperfectly, from a teleological search. The community
did not create these privileges of the Academy, any more than

the community created wisdom; rather, the community simply recognized the justice of the Academy's claim to privilege. The community did not expect to be served, except in the sense that it might be so fortunate as to gather some crumbs that fell from the academic table. Like Socrates and like Aquinas, the learned man, the teacher, was a servant of God wholly, and of God only. His freedom was sanctioned by an authority more than human. Now and then that freedom was violated, just as anointed kings were murdered or reverend priests were robbed, on occasion; yet it scarcely occurred to anyone to attempt to regulate or to suppress the freedom of the Academy; it was regarded almost as a part of the natural and unalterable order of things. Masters and scholars, moreover, were so jealous of their rights, and so ready to band together against any infringement upon their prescriptive prerogatives, that very great power and very great boldness were required for an invasion of the universities. This unity and this spirited defiance of the vulgar came, in considerable part, from the Schoolmen's conviction that they were Guardians of the Word, fulfilling a sacred function, and so secure in the right. In medieval times, it was precisely their "framework of certain key assumptions of Christian doctrine" that gave masters and students this high confidence. Far from repressing free discussion, this framework encouraged disputation of a heat and intensity almost unknown in universities nowadays— except possibly, among us, on certain political questions. Every medieval university had its colleges and parties and factions armed cap-à-pie—sometimes literally at sword's-point, or fife and drum ecclesiastic—against one another. They were free, these Schoolmen, free from external interference and free from a stifling internal conformity, because the whole purpose of the universities was the search after an enduring truth, beside which worldly aggrandizement was as nothing. They were free because they agreed on this one thing, if on nothing else, that the fear of God is the beginning of wisdom.

18

3

Only faint traces remain of the medieval university, Mr. Hutchins says, in our American university. "Every American university must justify itself in terms of the visible, tangible, material benefits that it confers upon the individuals who attend it and the community that supports it." The concept of a guild of teachers and scholars is withered away almost to nothing. "To Americans universities are businesses like every other element of this business civilization. Every business consists of employers and employees. The professors are employees. They operate within the framework of the American Way of Life and are subject to punishment for deviation from the popular view of that Way like any other members of the business community. Academic freedom is, I think, generally regarded as a device by which weak-minded or vicious people in some way hang on to their jobs when all right-thinking men would agree that they ought to lose them."[3]

This is harsh; yet the truth often is very harsh, in our time. And Mr. Hutchins thinks that matters have been thus ever since the beginnings of higher education in America. "The American university was not a corporation of students wanting to learn or teachers wanting to teach. It was a corporation formed by a religious denomination or by the state for the purposes of the denomination or state. The American university in the seventeenth century was much closer to the American university today than to the medieval university." Now I think that here Mr. Hutchins ignores one element common to the medieval university and to the American college, and that the most important of all elements: the teleological view of existence, and the religious function of the higher learning. As I have suggested earlier, the medieval university was not often a mere banding together of teachers or students; its real roots were in a cathedral school, or in an endowment for chantry priests who might spend much of their time in study and teaching. And the whole of its work was suffused with the belief that the fear of God is the beginning of wisdom. In this, the early American colleges were very like the medieval universities. As Mr. Hutchins himself remarks, the education of young men for the ministry was the chief motive for the founding of Harvard, Yale, Princeton, Brown, and so many other distinguished colleges. This dedication to religious principle is still the nominal reason, at least, for the existence of hundreds of colleges and universities endowed by religious bodies in America; nor has it been utterly lacking from our state institutions. A Catholic priest, Father Gabriel Richard, had much to do with the establishment of the University of Michigan; and the first president of that university, Henry Philip Tappan, a great educator, though very different in his theology from Newman, was quite as insistent as Newman upon the primacy of religious principle in true education:

> Man is a creature of passions and will, and therefore should be instructed in morality, and be disciplined to self-government. He is immortal, and therefore should he learn that system of religion which brings life and immortality to light.[4]

So Tappan wrote in 1851. Two years later, Newman wrote in his third discourse on University Education that the Utilitarian pedant, in ignoring the religious basis of education, leaves us all adrift: "The various busy world, spread out before our eyes, is physical, but it is more than physical; and, in making its actual system identical with his scientific analysis, such a Professor as I have imagined was betraying a want of philosophical depth, and an ignorance of what a University Teaching ought to be. He was no longer a teacher of liberal knowledge, but a narrow-minded bigot." Not merely the Catholic colleges in America, but the great majority of our institutions of higher learning, were founded upon tenets much like Tappan's and Newman's. I think that Mr. Hutchins does a disservice when he ignores this. For I believe that there is a direct connection between the concept of the scholar as the Bearer of the Word and the idea of academic freedom.

Before the Civil War, we hear little enough of academic freedom in the United States; but that does not suffice to substantiate Mr. Robert P. Ludlum's assertion that "until late in the nineteenth century there seems to have been a blithe disregard of academic freedom and tenure." The colleges—there were only two hundred and fifty, altogether, on the eve of the Civil War, and many of those were scarcely institutions of higher learning—except for the handful of state universities, were quite free of any sort of governmental interference, and so did not have much occasion for disputes in that quarter. Except for the state universities, every institution was supported by a religious denomination of well-defined views, and it was scarcely probable that a teacher would seek a position at a college hostile to his theological opinions; nor was he liable to question the right of such a college to discharge him for solitary dissent. The courses of instruction were comparatively few, and the classical languages, mathematics, and the other traditional disciplines were not calculated to provoke bitter controversy between professors and trustees. The aims of a college education were generally agreed upon, and professors and students generally were drawn from families and districts tolerably similar to one another. I am inclined to think, then, that the tranquillity of a century and more was the product of a common understanding, rather than of professors' pusillanimity and trustees' intolerance. Occasionally difficulties arose, as when, in 1820, public disapproval of Thomas Cooper's skepticism made his appointment to the faculty of the University of Virginia impossible, despite all that Jefferson could do in his behalf; and Thomas Jefferson himself once proposed to impose a republican political orthodoxy upon professors.[5] Yet no widespread problems of this sort occurred until the increasing heat of the Slavery Question was felt in the colleges, after 1830.

Oberlin, Western Reserve, Jefferson College in Mississippi, Centre College, the University of North Carolina, the College of South Carolina, Miami University, Kenyon College, Dickinson, Franklin, Harvard, the University of Georgia, Bowdoin, the University of Iowa, and Dartmouth College all experienced the dismissal of presidents or professors, during the three decades between 1833 and 1863, for views on slavery and secession. It could hardly have been otherwise: the issues were too close to ungovernable passions, and it is improbable that any other nation engaged in such a struggle would have behaved better. During the 'seventies and 'eighties, a number of professors were discharged—though most of them soon obtained chairs at other colleges—because they had in some degree espoused Darwinianism, to the vexation of the clergymen and farmers who still made up the majority of most boards of trustees. This controversy waned, however, and toward the end of the century the chief subjects in dispute were economic —reflecting, again, the temper of the age, and also the fact that manufacturers and entrepreneurs now were replacing the clergymen and farmers as college trustees.

The powers of college presidents, almost unlimited, and the zeal of trustees, met with no effectual opposition from teachers; and now the teaching of political economy, history, and sociology afforded a field for disagreement which had scarcely existed in the earlier history of American colleges. I do not propose to discuss here in any detail the cases—estimated to number between twelve and twenty-four—of serious disagreement between the administrators and the professors. Free silver, socialism, and related matters were the principal causes of these episodes between 1884 and 1914. After 1870, the direct influence of the German universities upon American higher education increasingly drew the attention of professors to the Germanic concept of "academic freedom", a phrase scarcely heard in this country earlier; and the widening breach between teachers and trustees over questions of political economy gave the idea immediate pertinence. Just what "academic freedom" meant at the German universities, not many Americans clearly understood: it was, in fact, almost wholly an internal freedom, the right to organize the curriculum without the interference of the minister of education; and it had been developed as a last safeguard against political meddling, in the secularized universities of the new bureaucratic German Empire. It was a tolerance by the state, rather than the assertion of a prescriptive right or a moral tradition; but American professors took up this German concept with more good-will than clarity of apprehension.

Whatever degree of vagueness enveloped the term "academic freedom" at the end of the nineteenth century, still scholars began to display some ability to defend their rights. When President Andrews of Brown University resigned over a disagreement with the governing board over the question of the coinage of silver, in 1897, very strong protests were made by scholars; and when Professor Edward A. Ross was forced out of Stanford University, in 1900, for similar reasons, certain of his colleagues protested and were compelled to resign. This affair was too dismaying to be tolerated; the American Economic Association investigated and sustained Dr. Ross. When Professor John M. Mecklin was compelled to resign from Lafayette College, in 1913, because of his view on biological evolution, the American Philosophical Association and the American Psychological Association protested. This concern on the part of the learned societies, spreading rapidly, led in 1915 to the formation of the American Association of University Professors—or, rather, was one of the principal causes for the establishment of that organization. Ever since then, Committee A of the Association has been the most active body interested in the defense of academic freedom. The reports of this Committee on Academic Freedom and Academic

Tenure, particularly its initial report in 1915, its statement of principles in 1925, and its amended statement of principles in 1940, constitute an index to the recent history of the concept in this country. The Committee has proceeded cautiously, aware that its only instrument for the defense of academic freedom is a reputation for moderation and thoroughness which may succeed in shaming violators of the principle into a reformation of their ways; and its statement of principles in 1950, drawn up by Professor W. T. Laprade of Duke University, is the best recent summary of the difficulties with which the question of academic freedom is beset at present. Although it has met with some harsh criticism, and I myself cannot agree with certain sentences in it, this statement is in general temperate and dignified, and I quote perhaps the most important passage here:

> Of the various freedoms essential if our society is to preserve itself and to promote the interests of the individuals that compose it, perhaps the most nearly absolute is that of scholars to direct their search for truth and to report the results of their findings. This freedom is immediately applicable only to a limited number of individuals, but it is profoundly important for the public at large. It safeguards the methods by which we explore the unknown and test the accepted. It may afford a key to open the way to remedies for bodily or social ills, or it may confirm our faith in the familiar. Its preservation is necessary if there is to be scholarship in any true sense of the word. The advantages accrue as much to the public as to the scholars themselves.[6]

To this statement there is appended a table of cases of alleged violations of academic freedom brought to the attention of the Committee between 1945 and 1950. On January 1, 1945, seventy-four cases still were pending from previous years. During 1945, the Committee dealt with 122 cases; in 1946, with 107 cases; in 1947, with 81 cases; in 1949, with 96 cases; in 1950, with 103 cases; in 1951, with 120 cases; in 1952, with 131 cases; in 1953, with 146 cases.[7] And it ought to be understood that many cases of infringement upon academic freedom never are appealed to this Committee—indeed, probably a great many more cases never are publicly discussed anywhere than the total number of those that come to the attention of the Association of University Professors. John Dewey, the first president of the Association, remarked at the first meeting of that body, in 1915, that he was confident that the topic of academic freedom "can not be more than an incident of the activities of the association in developing professional standards, standards which will be quite as scrupulous regarding the obligations imposed by freedom as jealous for freedom itself. The existence of publicly recognized and enforced standards would tend almost automatically to protect the freedom of the individual and to secure institutions against its abuse."[8] But the eleven cases brought to the attention of the Committee in 1915–16 contrast sharply with the multitude of invasions of academic freedom suggested by the preceding statistics of recent years. "Professional standards" have not sufficed to guarantee the freedom of the Academy; and the report of Committee A for 1952 (also prepared by Professor Laprade) reflects this sad truth:

> Some feel that the term academic freedom has become a stereotype, that it needs restatement in different words. Members of this Committee feel rather that the meaning of the term needs to be better understood and more widely supported. The public which maintains colleges and universities will defeat the achievement for which it hopes unless scholars and teachers are left undisturbed and free to do the work for which they were appointed.[9]

I may say here that I share the opinions thus expressed by Professor Laprade and his associates. I believe that the term "academic freedom" is not outmoded, nor the idea which it expresses. I believe that the term is often badly apprehended, and that the idea is insufficiently supported by either professors or the general public. I believe that both the mind of the scholar and the tone of society will suffer gravely unless the reality of academic freedom is intelligently and courageously sustained.* In the chapters which follow, I endeavor to take up some principal aspects of the question—aspects, often enough, which have been neglected in most of the discussion of such topics in the *Association of American University Professors Bulletin,* the journals of the learned societies, and the more popular press.

The reader who has borne with me to the end of this chapter will have gathered that I take academic freedom to be a valid idea, with both the sanction of an historically-defined meaning and the sanction of an enduring pertinence. Mr. Robert Hutchins believes that "The freedom of the modern university in a democratic society is based not on the remnants of a medieval tradition but on the proposition that societies require centers of independent thought and criticism if they are to progress or even to survive. Academic freedom means that the independence of the thought that goes on in a university is so important that a man cannot be restrained or punished by those who pay him because he holds views with

---

* A most interesting discrepancy exists between the statistics and opinions of Committee A of the Association of University Professors, and the statistics and opinions of the Commission on Academic Freedom and Academic Tenure of the Association of American Colleges. In its reports for 1951, 1952, and 1953, the latter body stated that not a single case of complaint concerning violation of the principles of academic freedom had been referred to it; and the report of March, 1952, drawn up by President Harwell G. Davis of Howard College, consisted chiefly of the following declaration (see *Association of American Colleges Bulletin,* March, 1952, and also the numbers for March, 1953, and March, 1954):

"Your Commission is encouraged to believe that there is an increasingly stronger conviction that the maintenance of these principles is essential not only to the integrity of our profession but also to enable us to render our most effective service to our God and our country."

Perhaps it is worth remarking that the AAUP is chiefly a body of university teachers, and the AAC chiefly a body of college and university administrators.

which those who pay him disagree."[9] For my part, I think that academic freedom, in our time, is founded *both* upon tradition and upon our present necessities. I do not think that academic freedom deserves preservation chiefly because it "serves the community", though this incidental function is important. I think, rather, that the principal importance of academic freedom is the opportunity it affords for the highest development of private reason and imagination, the improvement of mind and heart by the apprehension of Truth, whether or not that development is of any immediate use to "democratic society". And I find it impossible to concur wholly in the almost unlimited scope accorded to academic freedom by the definitions of Mr. Hook and Mr. Hutchins (though, in subsequent remarks, these gentlemen both acknowledge some limitations). Academic freedom, like every other prescriptive right, has its boundaries and its corresponding duties. When liberty declines into license, then it must be restrained; and if it is not restrained by those who enjoy that particular liberty, then it will be checked by other persons. There are times when the persons who pay a professor would be derelict in their duty if they did not endeavor to restrain the man who violates his own privileges; and, Professor Hook notwithstanding, it is prudent and necessary that there should sometimes exist a control upon the academy besides the control of what Mr. Hook considers "the rational methods by which truth is established." That such restraints may be very seldom exercised, it is important that the scholar and the teacher, recognizing the high duties of their vocation, understand clearly the solemn, and even holy, nature of the academy and its liberties. "The public has a right to expect candor of its servants," Mr. Norman Thomas writes, "emphatically including those who, as teachers, should inspire our youth in search of truth."[10] I understand what Mr. Thomas means; yet I hold that the scholar and the teacher, before thinking of what it is to be a servant, should think of what it is to be a man.

II

Intolerance and the
Educational Levellers

IN OUR AGE, Dean Inge remarked once, true freedom survives "only in the shadow-world of the intellectuals." If the shadow of freedom is to take on substance once more, probably the impulse must come from the Academy; Ideas, even in this time of Things, retain immense power. "Soon or late, it is ideas, not vested interests, which are dangerous for good or evil": so J. M. Keynes observes. It seems to me, then, that academic freedom, always valuable beyond price, has today an importance even greater than that it possessed in most ages—such an importance for human dignity and right reason as it possessed, in its rudimentary form, in the monasteries founded by Cassiodorus and St. Benedict. The universities of Salerno or Prague, Oxford or St. Andrews, if they experienced seasons of decline, in centuries long gone by, might be reinvigorated by the pulsating life in the society just without their gates, or might pass on their functions to other foundations. But I doubt whether there subsists within our present society, if our surviving centers of intellectual independence should go down to dusty death, the energy and the devotion required for a renewal of the true life of the mind. We live, when all is said, in the Iron Age. If the world is to

28

become once more aureate or argentine, every remnant of truly liberal understanding which may yet be found in our academies will be needed for the undertaking.

Though some of the outcry concerning the peril to academic freedom which we hear all about us is near to hysteria, in all of it is some grain of truth; and in a part of it is a great and sober truth. The statistics on the infringment of academic freedom which I have cited in the preceding chapter, however incomplete and susceptible of imperfect interpretation they may be, are some considerable proof that intolerance threatens now even the shadow-world of the intellectuals, with a ferocious power. The large majority of the cases appealed to the Association of University Professors are concerned with political questions, chiefly the reaction against radicalism—which reflects the obsession of our generation with politics, "the preoccupation of the quarter-educated." I deal with these political matters in a later chapter of this book. But there are other realms of intellectual liberty menaced quite as severely as political speculation, and very little has been said recently about these other realms, although they are at least as important to the human reason as pure or applied politics. Therefore I devote this chapter, and the one which follows, to some tentative discussion of two other aspects of the attack upon the Academy. The first of these is the intolerance of doctrinaire secularists and doctrinaire levellers in our colleges and universities; the second, the intolerance of certain professed guardians of tolerance and liberal opinion.

I have suggested already that the principal support to academic freedom, in the classical world, the medieval world, and the American educational tradition, has been the conviction, among scholars and teachers, that they are Bearers of the Word—dedicated men, whose first obligation is to Truth, and that a Truth derived from apprehension of an order more than natural or material. Such conviction is not yet ex-

tinct among us; and, as often enough in history men have
lived upon the intellectual and moral inheritance of earlier
times without acknowledging or even knowing the source of
their sustenance, so today a good many scholars and teachers
who think they have cast off the wisdom of their ancestors
nevertheless still draw their strength from disciplines and prescriptions which they profess to repudiate. The learned man of
integrity and courage among us, though he may deny the
Word, still draws his power from the Word. He may succeed
in convincing himself that the Word is a dead thing, or never
was alive; yet as it is a wise child, in debauched ages, who
knows his own father, just so nowadays even learned men
often experience the greatest difficulty in tracing back to its
high source the stream of reason and belief which keeps them
alive in the Wasteland.

Had there been no Voltaire (to borrow a witticism from
Mr. James Thurber's immortal Eliot Vereker) it would not
have been necessary to invent one; but without the religious
consecration which Voltaire's school ridiculed, there would
have been no learning among us, and no freedom; and if there
is to be no sense of religious consecration in the heart of the
professor of the next generation, soon there will be no professor, either. I do not mean to imply that a perfect religious
orthodoxy is necessary to modern learning or modern liberty.
So far as my private convictions have any bearing on this matter—and I trust that they have very little bearing—I am sufficiently heterodox to satisfy the most latitudinarian-minded
of my nonconformist ancestors. I do not happen to be a Catholic, or an Anglican, or a disciple of Dr. Niebuhr, or a colleague
of Mr. Aldous Huxley; doubtless that is my private misfortune. So far as I stand for any system of doctrines, I am an
archaic Puritan, which is much the same thing as a Gothic
Jew. My theological inclinations are worth no one's attention;
I mean only to suggest that, in this unlike my mentor Dr. Sam-
uel Johnson, heterodoxy is my doxy, not orthodoxy. But I am

of the opinion that the fountain of learning, and of liberty, is religion. I think that men who will not acknowledge the Author of their being have no sanction for truth, and that men who take this world for the only reality are (like the omnibus-passengers of Mr. C. S. Lewis' *Great Divorce*) actually in Hell, and that men who talk of "the dignity of man" without confessing that we derive that fleeting dignity from a yearning and an example more than human are bladders of wind. And I think that scholars—no matter how generous their intention—who would cut out religion and traditional morality from the academy, as Endicott cut out the Popish cross from his flag, would wound themselves, and all of us, to the heart. Dedication to an abiding Truth and to the spiritual aspirations of humanity excised, we would be left with no reason for learning, or for freedom, except service to "the people". And what is man, that we should serve him, except that man is made, however imperfectly, in the image of Another? The religious sanction gone, Caligula would be a wiser man than Marcus Aurelius. The pursuit of power and the gratification of concupiscence are the logical occupations of rational men in a world that is merely human and merely natural.

A scholar who finds himself unwilling to admit the existence of abiding Truth has only the alternative of dedicating himself to an ephemeral People, if he wants to have any motive in his vocation besides the gratification of the ego. Some of the most sincere partisans of academic freedom already have arrived at this embarrassing position. Professor Alexander Meiklejohn, for instance, a founder of the Association of University Professors, recently made the following curious profession of faith:

We, who engage in research and teaching, do so as agents of the people of the nation. In virtue of special abilities and training we are commissioned to carry on for the people forms of intellectual activity which belong to them, are done in their interest, but which, in some specific forms, they cannot carry on for themselves. Just as some men make shoes, and other men grow food, so it is our business to discover truth in its more intellectualized forms and to make it powerful in the guidance of the life of the community. And since we are thus acting as the agents of the people, they grant to us such of their freedom as is needed in that field of work. In a word, the final justification of our academic freedom is to be found, not in our purposes but in theirs. In the last resort, it is granted, not because we want it or enjoy it, but because those by whom we are commissioned need intellectual leadership in the thinking which a free society must do. May I state the principle bluntly and frankly? Our final responsibility, as scholars and teachers, is not to the truth. It is to the people who need the truth.[1]

Now I am sure that the people—though I dislike to have to consider persons as a collective abstraction—do need the truth; and in that sense, the scholars are a part of the people. But the people may not desire the truth, or at least the truth as interpreted by Professor Meiklejohn; the people may send Mr. McCarthy and Mr. Jenner, whose society Mr. Meiklejohn does not relish, to teach Professor Meiklejohn the popular version of this relative truth. If the people are the standard of right and the sole objects of learning, who shall say them nay? Their wish, their will, their want then become the absolute which Mr. Meiklejohn has sought to escape; and I am inclined to believe that Mr. Meiklejohn and his school will find this new Absolute not merely old Absolute writ large, but an exchange of King Log's domination for King Stork's domination. And if truth is only what serves the present interests of the multitude, who is to say that the people are wrong in what they want for themselves, and that Professor Meiklejohn knows their own interest better than they do? Quite possibly the people may derive greater satisfaction from the badgering of Dr. Meiklejohn's friends and colleagues than they would from the perusal of a treatise on nuclear physics; and in the Utilitarian scheme of ethics, other things being equal, pushpin is as good as poetry. I think that I, if only out of Utilitarian motives, would relish the service of the Truth more than the service of the People.

Nearly everyone who ventures to treat of the problems of academic freedom is fond of quoting from the *Apology;* and I shall do just that, preferring the authority of Socrates to my own feeble endeavors to suggest that Dr. Meiklejohn has got into waters more troubled than he knows. Socrates is on trial for his life; but life, for him, is a thing inferior to Truth:

> Men of Athens, I honor and love you; but I shall obey God rather than you, and while I have life and strength I shall never cease from the practice and teaching of philosophy, exhorting anyone whom I meet after my manner, and convincing him, saying: O my friend, why do you who are a citizen of the great and mighty and wise city of Athens care so much about laying up the greatest amount of money and honor and reputation, and so little about wisdom and truth and the greatest improvement of the soul, which you never regard or heed at all? Are you not ashamed of this? And if the person with whom I am arguing says: Yes, but I do care; I do not depart or let him go at once; I interrogate and examine and cross-examine him, and if I think that he has no virtue, but only says that he has, I reproach him with undervaluing the greater, and overvaluing the less. And this I should say to everyone whom I meet, young and old, citizen and alien, but especially to the citizens, inasmuch as they are my brethren. For this is the command of God, as I would have you know, and I believe that to this day no greater good has ever happened in the State than my service to the God. For I do nothing but go about persuading you all, old and young alike, not to take thought for your persons and your properties, but first and chiefly to take care about the greatest improvement of the soul.

For Socrates did not adhere to the opinion that he was simply commissioned as an agent of the people to serve them by "forms of intellectual activity which belong to them." It was not the people's purposes he was serving, or even his own, but the purposes of Truth, which generally is unpopular, and which never comes out of the masses, taken collectively. In the long run, the people not only of Athens, but of all the world, gained greatly from Socrates' intelligence, and even more from his integrity; but they would not have gained anything of the sort if he had worshipped Demos instead of God. Dr. Meiklejohn's friend John Dewey once declared that "Faith in the divine author and authority in which Western civilization confided, inherited ideas of the soul and its destiny, of fixed revelation ... have been made impossible for the cultivated mind of the Western world."[2] If it were true that Pragmatism had indeed made such beliefs impossible, then we might do very well to forget the example of Socrates, and abandon our foolish talk about human dignity and freedom and the high ordination of the teacher, and go over to the cult of Demos and the adulation of mediocrity and creature-comforts. But Pragmatism was the peculiar product of an infatuated epoch, and I do not think we need acknowledge this negation of philosophy as the consummate wisdom of the ages; its vogue is waning, and if we still hear its doctrines on every hand, that may be because (as Disraeli wrote) "prevailing opinions are generally the opinions of the generation that is passing." I think we need no longer be afraid to say, with Calhoun, "Democracy, as I understand and accept it, requires me to sacrifice myself *for* the masses, not *to* them. Who knows not that if you would save the people, you must often oppose them?"

One of the most heartening statements in opposition to the school of Professor Meiklejohn which I have come upon is contained in an address by President Douglas Knight of Lawrence College. He says, in substance, that the rejection of religious knowledge is the rejection of the human intellect, and of human freedom:

I am convinced of the necessity for this kind of religious awareness, which grasps experience in its multiplicity (rather than in some falsely-rationalized simplicity). The best attack upon the deep unreason, the sinister anti-intellectualism of our time, is an attack which grows from the full range of life rather than from desiccated rationality. And in this attack religion has a primary role to play. Secular humanism can at its best be merely defensive; it has no adequate place in its system for the full man—it recognizes him only in the guise of discursive intellect which at times he must assume. But religious humanism maintains the reasonable nature of man by the only means which stand a chance of victory; it refers him beyond himself to his ground and end in a livingly creative God. We have lost faith in the mind through a narrow and solipsistic view of its powers; now we must rediscover that faith by our rediscovery of the full universe within which and *only* within which the rational intellect can find its proper definition and use.[3]

During the past several years, I have made it part of my business to visit a good number of universities and colleges, with the intention, among other things, of trying to ascertain the degree of freedom of opinion and genuine searching after truth which prevails at institutions of various sorts. Now it has often been remarked, by gentlemen of varying social and educational opinions, that academic freedom commonly is more secure, and the unflinching pursuit of wisdom is more frequently encountered, at our distinguished private universities and colleges than at most institutions supported by the state; and I found this to be true. The necessity of conforming to popular impulses of the hour, as expressed through the executive and legislative branches of state governments, often severely hampers the independence of the state university or college, and sometimes even fixes the curriculum, in part, regardless of the judgment of the president and the faculty— for instance, the statute adopted in Michigan, last year, to prescribe the teaching of one year of political science to all students in all state institutions of higher learning. I do not mean to say that all state universities and colleges are weakly subservient to the political administration: one can find few faculties more independent than that of the University of Illinois, or few educational undertakings more boldly original than the University of California at Riverside. Nor do I say that all private colleges are havens of freedom of opinion: several have been severely censured, in recent years, by the Association of University Professors, and a tyrannical board of trustees or a bigoted president may very well impair the whole purpose even of a long-established and respectable private college. Yet, by and large, I am well enough satisfied that the atmosphere is freer, and the respect for the dignity of the professor greater, at private foundations. When one contrasts Harvard University with the University of Nevada, let us say, or Kenyon College with the Agricultural and Mechanical College of Texas, he becomes lost in wonder at the chain of reasoning of zealots for state-controlled education like Dr. James Bryant Conant.

Other reasons exist for this discrepancy than the responsibility of state foundations, directly or indirectly, to political authority. For one thing, an important motive for the establishment of state institutions of higher education, in all countries, has been the possibility of indoctrination in a social orthodoxy and of advancing the interests of the state as against the interests of voluntary associations and religious groups. Professor F. A. Hayek, in his *Counter-Revolution of Science,* describes dispassionately the development of the early polytechnic institutes, commencing in France, as agencies for centralized "social engineering" by the state—a deliberate transfer of the methods of physical engineering (suggested by a presumptuous scientism) to the control and direction of men in the mass. I cannot do better than to quote Mr. Hayek on the general tendency of these assumptions, which are at work among us with great power, and which tend to dominate, though only half-confessed and only imperfectly recognized even by their proponents, our state colleges of technology and, to a lesser extent, our state universities:

The great misfortune of our generation is that the direction which by the amazing progress of the natural sciences has been given to its interests is not one which assists us in comprehending the larger process of which as individuals we form merely a part or in appreciating how we constantly contribute to a common effort without either directing it or submitting to orders of others. To see this requires a kind of intellectual effort in which the traditional education in the "humanities" gave at least some practice, but for which the now predominant types of education seem less and less to prepare. The more our technical civilization advances and the more, therefore, the study of things as distinct from the study of men and their ideas qualifies for the more important and influential positions, the more significant becomes the gulf that separates two different types of mind: the one represented by the man whose supreme ambition is to turn the world round him into an enormous machine, every part of which, on his pressing a button, moves according to his design; and the other represented by the man whose main interest is the growth of the human mind in all its aspects, who in the study of history or literature, the arts or the law, has learned to see the individual as part of a process in which his contribution is not directed but spontaneous, and where he assists in the creation of something greater than he or any other single mind can ever plan for. It is this awareness of being part of a social process, and of the manner in which individual efforts interact, which the education solely in the Sciences or in technology seems so lamentably to fail to convey. It is not surprising that many of the more active minds among those so trained sooner or later react violently against the deficiencies of their education and develop a passion for imposing on society the order which they are unable to detect by the means with which they are familiar.[4]

The names of Dr. Robert Oppenheimer and Dr. Edward U. Condon, I think, may suggest sufficiently the sort of person that Professor Hayek has in mind here—a scholar in the physical sciences bent upon transferring (through a naïve analogy) power to manipulate nature into power to manipulate men. And this frame of prejudice, though operating upon persons far inferior in talents to Dr. Oppenheimer and Dr. Condon, produces at our state technological institutes an

37

alarming number of men of similar inclination; and, as Professor Hayek suggests, such was the deliberate intention of the early advocates of polytechnic instruction supervised by the state. It is a frame of prejudice innately hostile to freedom of mind and to the higher imagination.

Our state universities, though exempt to some degree from this tendency of the polytechnic college, nevertheless never have been wholly free from a proclivity toward indoctrinating students in the attitudes approved by current political authority. Even the earliest of them, founded by a man of liberal genius—the University of Virginia—experienced from the beginning this difficulty, not merely accepted, but actively urged, on occasion, by Jefferson himself (who would have had the professors required to teach pure republican doctrine out of approved textbooks, to squelch Federalism). It would be tedious, and would require too much space here, to recount the history of this tendency; it must suffice to say, just now, that every state university in America has suffered from it, though there has been much courageous opposition from professors and often from presidents to the compulsory teaching of a political orthodoxy among students. The private universities and colleges labor under no such compulsions; if they teach conformity to things as they are, still they do so for the most part voluntarily, or at least only under the compulsion of trustees who may differ among themselves on any board, and who certainly differ a good deal in their social convictions from one college or university to another. The private institutions, in short, have the inestimable advantages of diversity and of appeal to a select body of opinion, as contrasted with the dependence of the state institutions upon an executive or legislative political authority chosen by a mass of citizens inferior in education and discipline to the scholar and teacher.

And yet another reason for the superior degree of freedom enjoyed by professors in the better private universities and colleges is the sense of religious consecration which prevails in most of them. The links between churches and "denominational" colleges may have grown weak, in many instances; yet the belief that scholars are Bearers of the Word dies hard, in such places, and fortifies the professor against intimidation, and reminds the administrator that there are moral limitations upon his prerogative. Some private colleges of denominational affiliations, of course, exact conformity to a narrow doctrinal system; but these are much outnumbered by the Catholic, Episcopalian, Methodist, Lutheran, Dutch Reformed, Quaker, Presbyterian, Baptist, and other church-founded institutions which participate in a truly liberal view of learning. I do not say that these universities and colleges are perfectly free from acrimony and controversy, nor that they attain perfect justice in the relationship between trustees and faculties, or administrators and professors; of course they suffer incessantly from rancor and folly, as do all human institutions. But a sense that they are guardians of a Truth more than ephemeral, and that they are accountable to an Authority more than political, often produces a true tolerance denied to institutions avowedly secularistic. "On the whole," A. N. Whitehead observes, "tolerance is more often found in connection with a genial orthodoxy."

A well-known professor of history at a Jesuit university once told me that the formal constitution of such a foundation as that at which he taught, considered from an abstract view of academic dignity and self-governing institutions, was very bad. Modelled upon the quasi-military pattern of the Jesuit order itself (intended by St. Ignatius Loyola to inculcate obedience, rather than self-expression), and subject in theory to the absolute will of superiors in that order, such a university might be expected by anyone unfamiliar with its actual workings to be hostile to freedom of expression and repellent to the professor of independent character. Yet, in actuality, a very high degree of freedom of opinion prevailed in my friend's university, and the faculty was treated with a respect not often encountered in a good many secular foundations. Mistakes often were made, of course; petty intolerance and hauteur had to be expected, as at any other university; yet in the long run, no large or enduring injustice would be committed, my friend said; and that was more than he could say of other universities where he had taught. For the administrators of the institution were governed themselves by certain permanent and ascertainable rules of just conduct, and subject to the inspection of superior authority founded upon moral principle; reason was held in very high esteem precisely because its limitations, before Providence, were recognized; and the men of the cloth into whose charge the university was given were bound by solemn vows to the service of the Truth according to the light bestowed upon them.

In an admirably lucid lecture upon "Dogmatism and Tolerance", delivered at Rutgers University, M. Etienne Gilson explained this freedom of opinion in institutions governed by a set of religious convictions, which very often are especially receptive to truly liberal views and advanced opinions, political and philosophical:

> There is no necessary connection between philosophical dogmatism and political tyranny, no more than there is between philosophical skepticism and political liberty. How often have we not heard it said that if you are not tolerant in philosophy, you cannot be tolerant in politics! On the contrary, if I am a skeptic in philosophy, that is, if I am not sure of any particular philosophical truth, how could I be tolerant not only in politics but even in philosophy? We do not have to tolerate what we know to be right. We cannot even tolerate what we do not know for sure to be wrong. An intolerant skeptic would be a monster of perversity. It is only when we are certain that what somebody says or does is wrong, that we can judge it advisable to tolerate it. In short, where there is no dogmatism, there can be no tolerance, because there is nothing to tolerate. Tolerance does not consist in accepting all philosophical statements as more or less

probable, but, being absolutely certain that one of them is true and the others false, in letting everyone be free to speak his own mind. . . . Like any other moral vice, intolerance is a sin against the very nature of reason and one of the worst among the countless forms of stupidity. But precisely because intellectual light is his only weapon, a true philosopher cannot afford to be a skeptic with regard to the fundamental principles of human life. Now, when it comes to such problems, each of us has to be a true philosopher because his whole life is at stake. If you feel ready to surrender all your personal freedoms, you need not worry about philosophy because the State will soon tell you what to think; but if you are not yet ready for this fateful sacrifice, I could not too strongly advise you to take your philosophy seriously.[5]

It is no paradox, then, that educational institutions influenced strongly by religious dogmas often are most friendly to originality of thought and most mindful of the dignity of the scholar. If these religiously-influenced colleges and universities were to vanish, and only state-supported secular institutions should survive, the cause of academic freedom would be weakened almost to extinction. I think that academic freedom finds its fullest expression in foundations like the University of the South, an institution established and controlled by the Southern dioceses of the American Episcopal Church—indeed, the only college (theological seminaries excepted) in the United States directly supported by the Episcopalian Church. (The three other colleges with Episcopalian affiliations are private, as distinguished from churchly, establishments.) Some years ago, the faculty of the University of the South ousted their vice-chancellor (at Sewanee, as at the Scottish universities, the "president" of the institution) because of what they held to be his arbitrary ways; surely there are not many college faculties so intrepid and influential as this; and in a good many other particulars, freedom of expression flourishes at the University of the South—flourishes *because* of a religious view of life and thought, rather than in spite of that view. Two years ago, a fierce controversy took place at Sewanee: most of the members of the faculty of the divinity school demanded that the University publish a statement inviting negroes to enroll as theological students; and when the officers of the University protested that they had no right under the University's constitution, to issue such an announcement, the members of the divinity school's faculty resigned and went elsewhere. Without entering into the respective merits of the parties to this controversy, I may say that all this constituted not a violation of academic freedom, but instead a high example of what academic freedom ought to be. Whether or not the faculty of the divinity school were right and prudent in this stand, they stood by their professions intrepidly; and whether or not the officers and faculty of the University were right and prudent in their policy, they behaved with dignity and generosity, and held by their convictions without flinching before journalistic misinterpretation of the affair. The essence of academic freedom is that the scholar should have strong convictions, and stand by them, and that the academy should be governed by principle, and abide by principle. Sometimes, as in this instance, there will be conflict; without conflict, indeed, the academy would sink into ennui; but academic freedom is stimulated by conflict, if the struggle is part of a search for justice.

My opinion, then, is that religious conviction remains an indispensable support to academic freedom, and that an aggressive secularism, whatever words it may utter in praise of an academic freedom purely secularistic, is a menace to the academy's liberal functioning. Adherence to religious and ethical principles is far more likely to bring a true toleration than either a ferocious denial of these principles, or an indiscriminate welcome to every sort of proposal, which commonly degenerates into what Burke calls "a licentious toleration." Mr. Colin Clark, the influential Australian economist, writing in *Encounter*, reminds us of the disaster that can follow upon which President Chalmers of Kenyon College describes as "disintegrated liberalism"—that is, the liberalism which has disavowed belief in anything abiding, even in its own sources:

> It is surely a sign that the liberal philosophers have abandoned the very idea of objective truth when they refuse to condemn Marxism, or any other philosophy, and claim that the only purpose of universities is to maintain a sort of permanent debate on philosophical questions, without ever reaching or teaching any conclusions. How like the Sophism on which the Greek intellectual world foundered![6]

Now it is to American liberalism and American educational institutions that Mr. Clark is referring; and I share his vaticinations. I am depressed, therefore, when a scholar like Professor Sidney Hook, who has many sound things to say about academic freedom, opposes any study of religious knowledge as "authoritarian", and goes so far as to develop his own variety of bigotry with the dogmatic assertion that "there is no academic freedom in Catholic colleges"—which dictum, I am inclined to think, Mr. Hook probably would extend to any religiously-influenced educational institution that still adheres to dogmas and revealed truth.[7] I think that the triumph of this species of secularism would bring not intellectual emancipation, but the domination of another and far more repressive orthodoxy, to American education.

2

Like nature, the life of the mind abhors a vacuum. If the conviction that the scholar and teacher are Guardians of the Word trickles away, if the idea of higher education as a means to apprehension of an order transcending the fleeting present and the world of sensation is abandoned, if learning in college and university ceases to be (in Paul Elmer More's words) "a disciplining of the higher faculty of the imagination to the end that the student may behold, as it were in one sublime vision, the whole scale of being in its range from the lowest to the highest under the divine decree of order and subordination, without losing sight of the immutable veracity at the heart of all development, which 'is only the praise and surname of virtue' "—why, then, what is to replace these traditional concepts of the ends of education and the duties of the academy? A "scholarship" concerned only with the miscellaneous accumulation of facts, or with the kind of criticism which ignores values, or with mere utilitarian endeavors to extend man's mastery over nature, will repel and dismay the best minds of any era; the true scholars will sink into apathy or else turn their talents to action, rather than thought. And no society will long support and protect "scholars" of this ignoble pattern: having proved derelict in their duty of guiding the minds and hearts of mankind, the inhabitants of such an academy will be deprived of their academic freedom. Some aim or end the intellectual activity of any time must have, if it is not to expire of ennui. The more perceptive opponents of the traditional learning, knowing this, do their best to describe some pragmatic or positivistic ends for their new academy. And, substantially, they hope to supplant the "disciplining of the higher faculty of the imagination" by what they call "education for democracy."

This phrase is immensely popular. It is cherished, of course, by the disciples of John Dewey, both those belonging to the "adjustment-to-society" school and those ardent for "social reconstruction". It is the theme and title of that turgid document commonly known as the Report of the President's Commission on Higher Education (1948). Even Mr. Robert Hutchins and his friends, at least half the time, imply that such is the proper end of all our elaborate educational apparatus. It has penetrated to many colleges and universities originally dedicated to the principle that the fear of God is the beginning of wisdom. The very banality of the expression helps to insure its triumph. Who could be against education? And who could be against democracy? Yet the phrase begs two questions: What do you mean by "education"? and What do you mean by "democracy"? The school of Dewey has long been fond of capturing words and turning them to their own purposes: they tried hard to capture "humanism", and even laid siege to "religion." Now I am convinced that if, by "education," the champions of this slogan mean merely recreation, socialization, and a kind of custodial jurisdiction over young people, then they are deliberately perverting a word with a reasonably distinct historical meaning. And I am convinced that if by "democracy" they want us to understand "all things that are kindly and just and good", as they often seem to imply, again they are perverting an important word, with a reasonably distinct historical meaning, and making it into what Mr. Richard Weaver, in *The Ethics of Rhetoric*, calls a "god-term" —that is, a charismatic expression drained dry of any objective significance, but remaining an empty symbol intended to win unthinking applause.

Passing over the vast bulk of the writing on "education for democracy", lest I sink forever in that Serbonian bog, I propose to examine this concept briefly in the books of Professor Sidney Hook—not merely because Mr. Hook has written vigorously on the subject of academic freedom, but even more because his observations are immeasurably more lucid than most discussion of the subject, and his mind disdains shams. According to his lights, Dr. Hook tells the truth as he sees it, without equivocation and without mercy to his adversaries. He is in favor of genuine education, and he is in favor of genuine democracy; he does not want to convert our institutions of learning into mere juke-joints on a sumptuous scale, nor does he employ the word "democracy" as a blind for the totalitarian state governed by social engineers: he is quite as hard on "social reconstructionists" like Professor Theodore Brameld as he is on conservatives. Although still a professed Marxist in much, nevertheless he is a sincere American liberal (I do not pretend to be able to account for this insane conjunction) and sincerely devoted to American liberties. He is not a communist or a fellow-traveller; he perceived long before most other leftward-verging "liberals" did the frightful shape of Russian collectivism. He does not mince words, and he is not given to obscure verbiage. There is a good deal that I like about Professor Hook, in short, and if I single him out for attack here, it is because I think it only fair to criticize his school of thought at its strongest point.

Now Mr. Hook sees the necessity for ends in scholarship and formal education quite clearly. In *Education for Modern Man*, he draws up a list of seven ends, which, he thinks, will satisfy "most educators who are not open apologists for a political or religious church". With some minor reservations, I agree with these ends, and I suppose I am neither an open nor a secret apologist for a political or religious church: that is, as a conservative, I am a contemner of ideology and political indoctrination, and though a humble friend to religious principle, I am not a champion of any especial orthodoxy. My objection to Dr. Hook's list is that he touches upon only the minor ends of education, not the major ones; and, the major ends neglected, the minor ends are liable to degenerate into a system of thought, or absence of thought, that neither Professor Hook nor I would relish.

These are the aims of education, according to Mr. Hook: (1) Education should aim to develop the powers of critical, independent thought; (2) it should attempt to induce sensitiveness of perception, receptiveness to new ideas, imaginative sympathy with the experiences of others; (3) it should produce an awareness of the main streams of our cultural, literary and scientific traditions; (4) it should make available important bodies of knowledge concerning nature, society, ourselves, our country and its history; (5) it should strive to cultivate an intelligent loyalty to the ideals of the democratic community; (6) at some level, it should equip young men and women with the general skills and techniques and the special-ized knowledge which, together with the virtues and apti-tudes already mentioned, will make it possible for them to do some productive work related to their capacities and inter-ests; (7) it should strengthen those inner resources and traits of character which enable the individual, when necessary, to stand alone.[8] Now this would be a very thorough education, perhaps too thorough for everyone to take—thorough, that is, except for its neglect of certain grander elements which I shall mention presently. I think, however, that I can subscribe to every one of these aims, with the partial exception of the phrase "democratic community" in the fifth; for here Mr. Hook seems to postulate democracy as an absolute, every-where and at all times, regardless of particular circumstances. Yet if he simply means that these are ends for modern *Ameri-can* education, I would not disagree even here, provided that by "democracy" he means constitutional, representative, po-litical, traditional American democracy; I think, though, that he would have done better to have written "*just* community". And, incidentally, I object—impartially enough—to Mr. Hook's implicit exclusion of dogmatic political thinkers (I resort here to his own usage of the adjective "dogmatic") and of orthodox religious persons from the right to criticize these ends. If I were a Catholic, or a Jew, or an Episcopalian, or a Hindu, I think I still would be entitled to have something to say about the ends of education without being turned away as a hope-less fanatic.

What Mr. Hook ignores, however, is the grand function of the higher learning which I have tried to describe earlier: education as a liberating instrument which teaches us that we are part of some great continuity and essence more than material, and that life is worth living because there is more to life than mere physical existence. Mr. Hook leaves out of consideration what Unamuno calls "the tragic sense of life", the elements of grace, free will, and the contest against the evil woven into our nature; and without this, secular freedom leaves a man dry and restless, and academic freedom is a mere utilitarian device. Newman put it better than I can:

> In morals, as in physics, the stream cannot rise higher than its source. Christianity raises men from earth, for it comes from heaven; but human morality creeps, struts, or frets upon the earth's level, without wings to rise. The Knowledge School does not contemplate raising man above himself; it merely aims at disposing of his existing powers and tastes, as is most convenient, or as is practicable under circumstances. It finds him, like the victims of the French Tyrant, doubled up in a cage in which he can neither lie, stand, sit, nor kneel, and its highest desire is to find an attitude in which his unrest may be least. Or it finds him like some musical instrument, of great power and compass, but imperfect; from its very structure some keys must ever be out of tune, and its object, when ambition is highest, is to throw the *fault* of its nature where least it will be observed. It leaves man where it found him—man, and not an Angel—a sinner, and not a Saint; but it tries to make him look as much like what he is not as ever it can.[9]

Thus Newman against Sir Robert Peel, in his essay called "The Tamworth Reading Room", in 1841. Now I do not suppose that Newman hoped to convert Peel to his own views; and I have no hope of converting Mr. Hook. If this were a private argument between Professor Hook and your servant, all would be so much lost endeavor. For we touch here upon first principles, rooted in our earliest experiences and prejudices, probably in our unconscious selves, and conceivably in our inherited characters; we must not ask too much of poor defecated rationality. I think it impossible that I should succeed in changing Mr. Hook's mind on fundamentals, for we all have our dogmas, deny them though we will, and Professor Hook has his, "pragmatic" dogmas though they may be; and I, though still (like Sir Harry Vane) a Seeker, have a mind of so very different a cast from Professor Hook's that it is highly improbable that Mr. Hook could change it, whatever someone else might accomplish. But this is not a private argument between Mr. Hook and me, any more than Newman and Peel were engaged in a closed colloquy. The question just now is not so much whether Mr. Hook is right about the truth of religion or I am right, as it is this: Can there be an end or aim to anything without a religious interpretation of life? Are Mr. Hook's seven ends for education really true ends? May they not be minor ends, or possibly mere means to an end? Judging by the rest of Mr. Hook's *Education for Modern Man,* and by the bulk of his writings, Professor Hook himself feels a need for some larger and more satisfactory aspiration than simply "critical thought", or "receptiveness to new ideas", or "inner resources" *per se.* There is not much point in critical thought if thought itself is a mere function of the biological organism, nor much point in new ideas unless those ideas may lead somewhere, nor much point in inner resources if man has no inner yearnings. Somewhere there must exist an *object.* All men possessed of the higher imagination seek for such an object in existence. Religion is the instrument of that search. I think that all gifted men must have some sort of religion; and if they decline to accept traditional religion, then they set to work (often unwittingly) to manufacture their own religion. I think that Professor Hook has a religion. That religion is Democracy.

For Mr. Hook, as for his mentor John Dewey, Democracy is an absolute, an end in itself. "He is convinced that democracy can become a living faith for America in this age of social and scientific advance," says the jacket-description on *Education for Modern Man.* I repeat that we all have our absolutes, our dogmas, if we are reflective men, whether we acknowledge them or treat them as bastards. Democracy is indeed a living faith for Professor Hook—a religious faith. Demos is his god. I am aware that Mr. Hook endeavors to rationalize this emotional faith of his and to find utilitarian grounds for it, quite as certain persons who believe in a supernatural religion try to anthropomorphize their god and to obtain material proofs of his existence. Yet the very extravagance of his claims for Democracy suggest that Mr. Hook is in love not merely with a god-term, but with a god, the god Demos. Take, for instance, this sentence in *Education for Modern Man:* "A democracy is the only society which in principle believes that men can accept the truth in every realm of thought, and live with it."[10] Now Aquinas believed this, though he did not live in a democratic society, and was not a democrat; it was, indeed, the general assumption of the Schoolmen, in the feudal age. A scholar can make claims so extreme and unhistorical only if he is carried away by an emotion that transcends rationality—supposing he is sincere and frank, as I am sure Mr. Hook is. I suggest, then, that Mr. Hook is in the grip of private religious emotion whenever he writes of Democracy.

"It is possible to know God, if one does not try to understand him," Joubert says; and Mr. Hook, like John Dewey, follows this method with Demos—a faith that passeth all understanding. Now I take Demos for a false god, or at best a god with feet of clay, and therefore presume to try to understand what is meant, with reasonable accuracy, by the word Democracy. To Mr. Hook, as to a good many people, Democracy seems to incorporate Justice, Liberty, Charity, Loyalty, Equality, Honesty, and Lord knows how many other admirable qualities; Democracy is "a way of life", "a philosophy", "a living faith". It was so with Dewey, to whom Democracy was a moral value, almost *the* moral value. Again, Dewey endeavored to make this living faith, this religious conviction, conform somehow to his pragmatism: he maintained that Democracy was justified by its fruits. In Mr. Albert Lynd's summary of Dewey's position, "Democracy is a moral value because it is the social order which encourages each individual to make the most effective use of his powers for living with maximum satisfaction; or in the scientific view, to achieve the most successful relationship of the organism to its environment. Since the environment is so largely social, this adjustment cannot be achieved for individuals without social effort, that is, without the development of strong habits of co-operation."[11] But I think that Dewey's passion for Democracy was antecedent to this explanation of its virtues.

Mr. Hook himself, indeed, suggests that such is the invariable progress of faith in Democracy: first practice, then justification. That is precisely the method of religion: "Belief will follow action." Professor Hook seems to have taken his own medicine. Democracy is justified empirically, he contends, because "it makes for greater tranquillity, justice, freedom, security, creative diversity, reasonableness, and less cruelty, insensitiveness and intellectual intolerance than any other social system that has so far been devised or proposed."[12] The historical evidence for all this is shaky, at best, empirically speaking, I am afraid, and as Tocqueville suggests. Mr. Hook's praises might be nearer the mark if for "Democracy" he substituted Aristotle's polity, a blending of the best features of aristocracy and democracy, a counterbalancing of orders and interests, calculated to reconcile leadership and popular liberties, the rights of property and of persons. Once more, I venture to suggest that Mr. Hook adopts his faith first and finds his empirical evidence afterward. This, too, is a mark of all religions, or at least a dominant characteristic in the faith of most religious persons.

John Dewey arrived at his theory of the perfect virtue of Democracy by identical means. Mr. G. H. Bantock, writing in the *Cambridge Journal*, points out that Dewey actually judged his "process of living" in terms of an absolute, and that absolute was Democracy:

He tolerates, however, only one type of social organization—the democratic, a state of society which he nowhere defines with any clarity, nor indicates in detail how democratic government is to manifest itself. His conception of it is partly emotional—he equates it generally with anti-authoritarianism, and sees in it a bulwark against privilege and exploitation. Perhaps the nearest he gets to definition is when he asserts that "a democracy is more than a form of government; it is primarily a mode of associated living, of conjoint communicated experience." The two most important elements of democracy to which he points are: "more numerous and more varied points of shared common interest [and] greater reliance upon the recognition of mutual interests as a factor in social control" and "freer interaction between social groups . . . [and] change in social habit—its continuous readjustment through meeting the new situations produced by varied intercourse." It is here that the two chief elements in Dewey's system meet. For it is quite obvious that however much Dewey advocates the necessity of constant change, of continual reconstruction of experience, that change must work *within* the democratic framework, and no changes in social habit which will in any way endanger this "mode of associated living" are to be permitted. Indeed, it is an indication of Dewey's naïvety that he rarely seems to conceive the possibility of its happening.[13]

Certain of Dewey's claims for Democracy, summarized above, are very like Engels' claims for Communism. What Dewey, however dimly, seems to have in mind when he uses the word "Democracy" is really not the political tradition with which we associate that word, but instead a utopian collectivism, in which everyone shall be just like everyone else—indeed, as in Huxley's *Brave New World,* everyone shall belong to everyone else. As Mr. Bantock suggests later, this concept of Democracy involves the extinction of strong personalities and unusual talents. I am inclined to think that it might go still further, all the way to Mr. C. S. Lewis' *Abolition of Man.*

If I sound extreme, consider this passage from Dewey's *Democracy and Education,* concerned with a levelling of character and intellect in the name of Democracy which would sound perfectly appropriate if inserted into the "Newspeak" passages in Orwell's *Nineteen-Eighty-Four.*

Dewey denounces "the false conception of culture which iden-
tifies it with something purely 'inner' ";

> And the idea of perfecting an "inner" personality is a sure sign
> of social divisions. What is called inner is simply that which does
> not connect with others—which is not capable of free and full
> communication. What is termed spiritual culture has usually
> been futile, with something rotten about it, just because it has
> been conceived as a thing which a man might have internally—
> and therefore exclusively.[14]

Here is reflected a collectivism, a classless society, which out-
does Marx; not even property in the inner life of the spirit
is to be left to the human person in Dewey's Democracy.

Now I do not mean that Dewey, or Mr. Hook, intend to reduce us to a condition less than human. Even professors of
philosophy do not always foresee the long-run consequences
of their theories. Mr. Hook, like Dewey, is a humane man,
and doubtless would be one of the first to take an intrepid
stand against an immediate menace to American liberties,
whether of the body or of the mind. But I think that Dewey
and Hook are better than their theories. Reared in the freedom
of American society, they early became attached to democracy
as an ideal, and in time made Democracy into an abstraction
and an absolute, for lack of any other god. I do not wish to
deprive Mr. Hook of his religion; I am sure that it makes him
a better man. But I object to his preaching this private religion
of his to the world, as a substitute for traditional and supernatural religion, because really his god is only a little graven
image. Democracy is not a god, or a "way of life", or a philosophy, or a living faith. Democracy is a word. That word means
a political community in which the will of the majority rules.
Democracy is not an absolute, or an end in itself, but a means
to certain ends. Chief among those ends are Justice and Freedom. When Democracy sustains Justice and Freedom, then
Democracy is praiseworthy; when it overthrows Justice and

Freedom, then Democracy is evil. At various times in history, Democracy has been a good, and at other times it has been a curse. Its efficacy depends upon many factors—the state of education among a people, the distribution of property, the influence of religious belief, the nature of the political constitution, the absence or presence of counterbalancing elements in the polity, the moral character of leadership. Pure democracy—that is, direct exercise of the powers of government by the mass of people, at all times—is impossible in complex modern states, and functioned disastrously even in Athens. I am more than willing to agree with Mr. Hook that our traditional American democracy—a mixed government, really, with representative institutions, written constitutions, the system of political checks and balances, and a long record of valuable experience—is the very best government that the United States can expect; it is sanctioned by prescription. I feel sure that Mr. Hook is sincerely attached to this American government. But when he, like Dewey, abstracts the word "Democracy" from this practical, balanced, traditional constitution of our country, and claps it, as a god-term, upon a quite different concept of a collectivistic society, in which everybody belongs to everybody else, I refuse to follow him. I agree with him that Democracy is not the product of Christianity, any more than Monarchy is, or Aristocracy; Christianity prescribes no especial form of politics. Democracy, I repeat, is simply a means to certain ends, and sometimes those ends may be attained by other means. And those ends, Justice and Freedom, *are* in large measure the products of religious faith, of the religious conviction that the human person has dignity and rights because divine wisdom so ordained. Therefore I think it would be perilous in the extreme to substitute the cult of Demos for the religious convictions which have raised man from the state of nature, "poor, nasty, brutish, and short," to the civil social existence of Justice and Freedom. I do not think that academic freedom could long prosper under King

Demos, if Democracy should succeed in casting off its religious sanctions. I turn to Mr. Bantock's penetrating article again:

> Dewey's influence is, then, to be observed in many of the more questionable aspects of current educational policy: the decay of a concern for values; the increasing "socialization" of education, with the consequent decline in respect for academic standards it implies; the depreciation of such aspects of knowledge as do not permit of immediate utilization in the world of practical activity and the restriction of educational aims thus involved; the foolish or disingenuous appeal to scientific criteria as the sole test of human "truth"; the current reluctance to accept the idea of the objectivity and "authority" of knowledge. But there is a still greater danger. For, by introducing the ethos of "mass-man" into the traditional curricula of the learned, Dewey represents a threat to the whole tradition of European learning.[15]

Professor Hook is staunchly opposed to indoctrinating students in "Democracy", or in anything else. Democracy, he says, cannot successfully be reduced to abstract doctrine, and I agree. With his accustomed vehemence, he attacks Professor Meiklejohn for asserting that "the purpose of all teaching is to express the cultural authority of the group by which the teaching is given" (repudiating, at the same time, "these Hegelian notions", by which John Dewey was strongly influenced); and he pours the vials of his wrath upon "a group of educators who had substituted a paternalistic conception of welfare for the vision of democratic mutualism and political liberty central to progressive education."[16] In short, Mr. Hook is a genuine democrat, and a force for good in America. Personally, he is nobly tolerant, and I feel certain that were I to teach under him, I would enjoy the greatest freedom of expression, though he would disagree with two-thirds of what I might say. How true a disciple of John Dewey he remains— why, that is another matter altogether; he thinks he is the pure Deweyite, as he is the pure Marxist, and that Professor

Brameld and the "social reconstructionists", like Lenin and Stalin, are heretics or schismatics from the good old cause. I do not have much confidence in his logic, here; but it is better to be true to Truth than to an old master, or to Demos; and, according to the light that is given him, Professor Hook is constant to Truth. He is a man worthy of academic freedom. But I think he apprehends insufficiently the dangerous tendency of some of Dewey's doctrines and some of his own. I have gone into this matter at some length because Dewey was a prime mover in the definition and protection of academic freedom in this century, and because Mr. Hook had carried on that cause with resolution. All the good intentions in the world, however, may only be utilized as so many paving-stones in Hell, if they are unaccompanied by right reason. The preservation of academic freedom in our time of troubles requires the most candid criticism of the idea itself. President Knight of Lawrence College puts the difficulty with some force:

We face, then, a situation in which both society and the universities are confused about basic standards of value. Beyond all the pressure by which outward events of the last two generations urge us toward fear-conditioned judgments about security stands a basic bewilderment. This bewilderment involves the basic nature of democracy; it has been developing for as long as our American culture, and (as we can now recognize) it has perhaps been an inseparable part of that culture. As we have become steadily more secular in our conception of a way of life, we have come more and more to call into question an individualist concept of democracy and to replace it with something closer to the root meaning of the word but farther from our own best interests—a kind of mass government where half-education and semi-literacy can be played upon by a shrewd combination of fear and seduction. We are producing an electorate which is educated just well enough so that it can be easily victimized by mass propaganda. The anti-intellectualism which is our particular concern as educators seems to me to be only one aspect of an anti-responsibility of which all of us tend to be victims, whether we suffer it in a crude or a learned form.[16]

A degradation of the democratic dogma is indeed at the root of the present distresses of academic freedom in America. Burke and Newman, as well as John Dewey, believed in employing the empirical method, so that principle, in any particular circumstance, might be guided by prudence. To descend from the abstract to the particular, then, I shall now take up in detail perhaps the most shocking case of the violation of academic freedom in many years, an affront to justice which Professor Hook himself, at least in private, condemned wholeheartedly. And I propose to show that this saddening episode in an American university was directly related to those notions of "democracy" and "equality" and "progressive education" which Mr. Hook expounds. Although an examination of consequences is not the only method for judging the truth of a principle, it is Mr. Hook's way, and John Dewey's. I intend to apply that method here. I know that Hook or Dewey, had they been in a position of authority, would have acted very differently from the person responsible for the affair I am about to describe; but the prudence of embarking upon any mass-movement must be predicated upon the character of the average sensual man, not upon the high-minded character and intentions of the doctrinaires who first advocated the repudiation of tradition and authority.

3

The subject of academic freedom cannot be separated from the subject of academic standards: for the professor is respected, and respects himself, because he is the master of a high discipline and the teacher of a traditional and valuable body of knowledge; he is a keeper of a people's wisdom; he is the servant of the Truth, and of the Truth only. If he lowers his standards of learning, or is forced to lower them; if he becomes an indoctrinator, rather than a professor of arts or sciences, or is compelled to indoctrinate his students; if, instead of teaching students who respect him and his discipline, he is expected to contend with so many wild beasts at Ephesus, who despise pure learning and resent any endeavor to create a taste for learning—why, then he will lose the respect of society, and he will lose his own sense of honor and dignity. I propose to touch upon this matter further in my concluding chapter. Just now I mean only to suggest its pertinence in the case I am about to describe.

Since the end of the Second World War, at nearly all American colleges and universities an eagerness has been manifest for the lowering of admission-requirements and of standards of performance expected of students. The jamming of colleges with veterans entitled to governmental assistance provided an initial excuse for waiving requirements of scholarship; then, some college and university professors becoming intoxicated with aggrandizement and indulging a latent passion for confounding quality with quantity, too many colleges endeavored to maintain enrollments at their 1947–1950 peak by giving permanence to the emergency standards—thus attracting students to the campus who might not have been tolerated there before 1942. In the beginning, this affection for swollen enrollments was confined to "administrators": the true professors, overworked and exasperated at the apathy of the new student-body, would have been happy to have returned to the quieter days of 1930 or 1940. But gradually the administrators won over to the cause of aggrandizement a large number of the professors. Salaries, they insisted, would not rise unless enrollments rose; nor would promotions be frequent; and, after all, what did it matter? If the president and the dean were willing to break with tradition, how could a mere inefficient professor of arts or sciences presume to object?

By 1953, at possibly the majority of American institutions of higher learning, the process of lowering standards was far advanced. The degradation, indeed, was elevated by its apologists to the dignity of a principle, and the authority of John Dewey was cited time and time again in its support. The authors of *Higher Education for American Democracy* (1947) had urged educators to admit a vastly larger proportion of young people, at whatever cost to learning, in the name of "democratic living". Here and there, nevertheless, a college courageously defied this great blind tendency; now and then the head of an institution (Mr. Hutchins, or President Chalmers of Kenyon, or President Dodds of Princeton) analyzed its fallacies; and at every university and college, no matter how far advanced the disease of adulterated learning, there remained at least a few professors of attainment who strove to arrest this manifestation of "progress". Their situation, on some campuses, became increasingly difficult. Were they fighting a rear-guard action? they began to ask themselves. Or were they, in reality, already in the concentration-camp, mocked by administrators and educationists and despised by the students, or most of the students? And if their own consciences were not enough to contend with, presently the hierarchy of the university itself often began to scowl upon them because they had not yet surrendered themselves to the "wave of the future" and continued to cling obdurately to some tattered notions of academic dignity and decency. For was not all this change in the interest of Democracy? Were not colleges and universities established to serve the People?

Perhaps the most illuminating instance of this struggle between vulgarization and standards occurred at the University of Nevada, in 1952–1953. Other cases almost as dismaying may have happened elsewhere; indeed, I am sure that they did; but ordinarily the administration of a college is able to prevent the public from getting wind of the affair, or else the scholar involved thinks it more prudent to submit in silence. He has a future to think of, after all; and many professors take a positive relish in talking of their "hostages to fortune".

The Nevada case may be said to have begun in August, 1952, when Dr. Frank Richardson, associate professor of biology at the University of Nevada, a mild-mannered and amiable ornithologist, read an article by Professor Arthur Bestor, professor of history at the University of Illinois, entitled "Aimlessness in Education", which was published in *The Scientific Monthly*. Not until the autumn of 1952, however, did the other elements which caused the trouble at Reno make their appearance. The chief of these elements was Mr. Minard W. Stout, a doctor of education (whose thesis, at the University of Iowa, had been entitled "The Administration of the Extra-Class Activity Finances in Iowa High Schools during the School Year of 1941–42") newly elevated to the presidency of the University of Nevada. Previously, Mr. Stout had been principal of the University High School of the University of Minnesota. A zealous educationist, he set about tightening his presidential grip upon things at Reno, and soon announced a program for reducing entrance-requirements.

Professor Richardson, who had spent eleven years at the University of Nevada, was elected president of the Nevada chapter of the American Association of University Professors about the time that Mr. Stout took up his presidential duties. Popular with his colleagues and with students, he held permanent tenure in the University, was head of his department, and had been appointed to the chairmanship of responsible committees. Well before Dr. Stout had come to Reno, Professor Richardson had written to Illinois to obtain thirty reprints of "Aimlessness in Education",* Dr. Bestor's shrewd criticism

---

* A book grew out of Dr. Bestor's article: a very good and penetrating book, his *Educational Wastelands*, published by the University of Illinois Press. The efforts of the professional educationists, at Illinois and elsewhere, to suppress this moderate and scholarly book can only be described as frantic; but the Press and the faculty did not give way to this pressure, which is a great deal more than can be said of many universities. The book has begun to assert a wide influence, despite the infuriated reviews written by professors of education which appeared in many journals.

of the decay of regular disciplines in American colleges; and, receiving these copies in November and thinking that the essay would be of as much interest to his colleagues as to himself, Dr. Richardson sent reprints to a number of them. To the new president, also, he sent a copy, with a conciliatory note attached, as a matter of form. That little act of civility set off an explosion.

A statement subsequently drawn up by Dr. Richardson's friends describes the course of events that had immediately preceded this explosion:

> During the week of the fall opening of the University of Nevada for the academic year 1952-53, President Stout, making his first appearance before a general faculty meeting, spoke informally and from notes, on his conception of university organization and administration. The only remarks which seemed to cause any particular speculation among members of the faculty were those which suggested the possible abolition, or reduction to a mere advisory capacity, of the faculty committees then in existence, and the establishment of what the President termed a "Chain of Command." The latter seemed to stay within the framework of administration already operative, i.e., the Board of Regents; the President; the Deans of the Colleges; the Chairmen of the Departments; all instructional personnel; but a good many, reading a new formality of almost military rigidity into a presentation which otherwise, since it made no outward changes, seemed scarcely worth making, feared that a serious reduction of the democratic ease and informality of proceedings, left by President Malcolm Love, was threatened.

President Stout soon went further. He made it clear that he was an educational imperialist, intent upon enlarging greatly the enrollment in the University; and to this end, with the consent of the Regents but disregarding all protests of the faculty and their established committees, he drastically lowered the requirements for entrance. Henceforth (after April 10, 1953) all graduates of Nevada high schools, regardless of their academic standing or of the subjects they had studied, might enroll in the University without impediment. Now Dr. Richardson was chairman of the faculty committee on scholastic standing, handling all probations and suspensions of students; and so, he writes, "This sort of thing bothered me, especially since I was so close to all the unhappiness connected with suspension of students, many of whom should not have been admitted in the first place."

The new president of the University of Nevada liked neither Professor Richardson's criticisms of a policy of abolishing entrance-standards, nor his presuming to distribute copies of an article opposed to the educationist doctrines in which Mr. Stout had been schooled. In November, Dr. Richardson was summoned to a conference with President Stout, Dean Frederick Wood, and Dr. Harold Brown, head of the department of education. A stenographic report of this interrogation was kept, and later became a most important document in the Nevada Supreme Court's review of the case; it is an interesting specimen of an attempt by an "administrator" of the new sort to bully an educated gentleman of scientific discipline. The following extracts from the record of the conference (November 19, 1952) may suggest the sort of mind and temper possessed by too many educational administrators recruited from the schools of education, the technicians of teaching, trained in the orthodoxy of latter-day Deweyism, and remarkably ignorant of almost any branch of what they contemptuously call "subject-matter".

PRESIDENT STOUT: I called this meeting to consider something which I feel is very serious. I was the one who called the meeting—no one else did. (Refers to the article "Aimlessness in Education" which Dr. Richardson had circulated among the faculty.) I am concerned because of the criticism regarding one of the departments of the university. Do you consider this Dr. Arthur E. Bestor, Jr., to be an authority in the field of education?

DR. RICHARDSON: I don't know him personally, of course. I do know the *Scientific Monthly* and think the quality of its articles is always excellent, so I was assuming that he was well qualified to write.

. . .

STOUT: Is there anything that makes him an authority in the field of education?

RICHARDSON: I didn't worry about that because he is dealing with a subject that people should be concerned with whether they are authorities or not. He is dealing with a subject we are all interested in.

STOUT: You mean there are areas you can know without any previous training?

RICHARDSON: You can recognize the areas we should be thinking about without being an authority in the field itself.

. . .

STOUT: Here is a problem in education, public school education. An article comes out written by this person. You have no information except what it says at the head of the article. You accept what he says as being a good answer to the extent that you order copies and distribute them to a number of the faculty. Now my question is, "Is that an example of your practice at scientific thinking and action?"

RICHARDSON: Well, I think so. I certainly didn't make any claims for this article and I am still perfectly willing to recognize that it is onesided in many ways, but I know that many of the faculty were interested in this matter and that many would not have had a chance to see it. I would have been willing to distribute articles on the other side, too. . . . In the first place, it was of interest because two years ago we went through considerable discussion on the subject when high-school curricula were discussed.

STOUT: Were you in on that—where you posed as an authority as to what is good in high school? Were you trained in high school curricula?

RICHARDSON: No.

STOUT: Did you accept the assignment?

RICHARDSON: I did.

STOUT: Have you had any training in science programs for high school students?

RICHARDSON: I have had some knowledge of them.

STOUT: Answer my question—any training?

RICHARDSON: Well, that depends—you mean courses? I have had education courses.

STOUT: Any course in science education?

RICHARDSON: No.

STOUT: Have you ever taught in a high school?

RICHARDSON: No, but I am still very much interested and concerned.

STOUT: There are many people who are concerned about the field of biology who have had no training in it. Would you accept their recommendation about what should be done in biology?

RICHARDSON: I surely would listen to them.

. . .

STOUT: Dr. Richardson, this is serious, because on this campus there is not going to be any departmental friction. There is going to be no case of any departmental *belittling* or criticizing others. In case there is any individual who feels he has to stir it up, then he is going to leave the faculty. In case there are two people who can't get along, both of them will go. I want it very clear that this instance has caused me to lose a great deal of confidence in your judgment. At this time I have grave doubt that you have the judgment to serve as department head in this university, because I can see no evidence of it in this case. I want it very clear that there is not to be another instance like this either above board or under cover. You were hired to teach biology. This year you were given the appointment to serve as department head. That does not make you a critic or a supervisor of the entire program of higher education. As I said in the opening faculty meeting, I believe in having experts who know their fields and who have the judgment to stick to their fields. It may be that you can't be happy here working under that condition, but that is the decision you will have to make. But, under no condition is there going to be any belittling of other departments or faculty members. Have I made myself clear?

RICHARDSON: May I speak for myself? I started to tell you why I thought this article was of interest to me. It was based on the fact, partly, because we have discussed the matter in the past, also because it concerns the subject of admission requirements which we have been discussing recently. That is a subject of vital interest to the whole faculty. It does not involve any particular person. It involves us all here. I did not have the department of education in mind here and I think there is no indication that I had them in mind when I sent this article out.

STOUT: You should not have said that, because that does not improve my opinion of you. . . . Aren't there some unsolved problems in the field of biology that would keep you busy, and leave other problems to other people?

RICHARDSON: I have to be concerned with admission requirements. I am interested in my own children's education and the students in my classes.

STOUT: Frankly, it is none of your business. That rests in the hands of the Regents.

RICHARDSON: It does affect me in many ways, however—the quality of students and their attitudes. I am necessarily concerned.

STOUT: We are not going into that discussion because, as I said, you are hired to teach biology and not to be a buttinsky all over the campus. Dean Wood is responsible for all the college of liberal arts. I have confidence that he can handle that. If you handle the department of biology as it should be handled, I think you will have your hands full. Otherwise, Mr. Richardson, something else will have to be done. I may be a little more blunt than some people have been in the past, but I think certain things have been pointed out to you in the past and I just don't believe in fooling around. If you are not happy in the job that is assigned to you, we will help you move, but as long as you stay here, we will ask you for help in other areas when we need it. That is all.

The brutal and vulgar language of President Stout somehow does not seem to be inconsonant with a professed devotion to "education for democracy": such persons often have the word "democracy" in their mouths, and defend their plans for aggrandizement and disregard of standards by an appeal to "education for all the people." The vagueness of Dewey, and even of Dr. Hook, in defining democracy leaves educationists of Mr. Stout's school free to employ that god-term as they please.

President Stout, in fine, was not the man to tolerate qualms of conscience. In the bill of particulars which the Board of

Regents later was compelled to file with the Supreme Court of Nevada, Mr. Stout describes his own annoyance at having to endure the distribution of copies of "Aimlessness in Education" by this pestilent professor. On March 31, 1953, Mr. Stout sent to Dr. Richardson and four other members of the faculty a letter the tone of which may be sufficiently suggested by the following extracts:

Grave concern is growing in the minds of many people concerning the harm being done to the morale of the staff as well as to the welfare and reputation of the University by a small dissatisfied minority group in the faculty of the University. The disturbing activities of this group, which have extended over several years, have included this year:

1. The attempt to develop friction between departments on the campus.

2. The attempt to develop friction between the University and the public schools of the State.

3. The spreading of false information to infer the abolishment of many faculty committees.

4. The spreading of false information to infer the lowering of academic standards at the University.

5. The spreading of false information to infer the maltreatment of faculty members by the administration.

6. The alarming of faculty, townspeople, and legislators without first presenting the matter to the administration directly or to the Faculty Welfare Committee which is elected by the faculty members to handle such matters with the administration.

. . .

It is known to the Board of Regents that you are a member of this small dissatisfied minority group.

Therefore, you are requested to appear for a hearing before the Board of Regents in the President's office at 11:30 A.M. on April 10, 1953, to explain your participation in the activities of this group and to show cause as to why you should be continued as a member of the faculty of the University of Nevada beyond June 30, 1953.

Upon receiving this remarkable communication, Dr. Richardson and the others threatened took legal counsel. Three of

66

the five accused, after they had promised loyalty to the president, were left unmolested, though unsure of their ultimate future; a fourth, Dr. Thomas W. Little, assistant professor of biology and vice-president of the Nevada chapter of the AAUP, was compelled to resign (despite the nominal dropping of charges against him) by the mockery of a re-appointment at a salary less than that of his own assistant; and thereafter the detestation of the President and Regents was concentrated against Dr. Richardson. Possessing tenure, he could not be dismissed "except for cause and after a hearing before the Board of Regents."

Such a hearing was on May 25, 1953, and it was nearly as thorough a mockery of justice as the interrogation by President Stout quoted at length above. The Regents all were opposed to any form of faculty independence, and apparently were now resolved to crush it once and for all by making an example of Richardson. Most members of the Board of Regents were businessmen, in a small way—an undertaker, a hotelkeeper, and others; like many such boards at state institutions, they were elected by popular vote, and ordinarily nominated by their party as a reward for services or contributions to the party. It soon became clear that not one member of this Board had the least concept of academic freedom, nor indeed of the elementary rules of justice. The Board sat both as accuser and as judge. No specific charge ever was brought against Dr. Richardson: he simply was commanded to defend himself (with the burden of proof resting on his shoulders) against general allegations of having been insubordinate, uncooperative, and "not in accord with the welfare of the University of Nevada." He was allotted thirty minutes for whatever defense he might undertake against charges the content of which he did not know. The parallel with Russian political purges is too strong to go unmentioned. "I'll be judge, I'll be jury,/Cried the cunning old Fury."

Before this hearing took place, however, the Regents had

been compelled by an order from the Supreme Court of Nevada to present a bill of particulars against the accused. These particulars were simply the sweeping charges of insubordination and uncooperativeness which are mentioned above; but Dr. Richardson was compelled to undergo the investigations of this curious tribunal. One of the Regents subsequently remarked that though it was a pity to lose Dr. Richardson, it would have been worse to have lost Dr. Stout; another, an aspirant after the gubernatorial chair of Nevada, was hotly opposed to any compromise. Not a single member of the Board was a man of intellectual eminence; while only two were trained in any scholarly or professional discipline. The verdict was foregone. In the course of the hearing, the chairman of the department of education, Dr. Brown, testified that he had been told by Dean Wood that he had "best cooperate" by making his statements unfavorable to Dr. Richardson—which, however, he refused to do. (Dr. Brown was subsequently passed over in the appointment to a deanship for which he had been the leading candidate.) At the end of the hearing, Dr. Richardson was dismissed from the University. "Those who supported Richardson," one of his most active friends said, "were shocked to conclude that the only doctrine emerging from his case was the one that a professor at Nevada dare not disagree in any way with the Regents and administration. Nor did it help matters that the Regents, on announcing Richardson's dismissal, gravely protested that freedom of expression at the university was inviolate."

Although Dr. Richardson, with his family, departed for Hawaii to study sea-birds for a year, the lawyers who had volunteered to defend him and Dr. Little carried his case to the Supreme Court of Nevada. Assuming jurisdiction through a writ of certiorari in September, 1953, the Court denied the Regents' request for a dismissal and stated that the Regents must be bound by the ordinary rules of procedure governing administrative bodies acting in a judicial capacity, and by their own announced tenure-policies. The decision in this case was not reached for seven months. Meanwhile, Dr. Walter Van Tilburg Clark, the novelist and professor of English, resigned from the University of Nevada in protest against the treatment of Dr. Richardson. Stern protests against the injustice of the dismissal were sent to the University of Nevada by many faculty members of the University of Illinois, by a similar group at the University of California, and by the chapter of the AAUP at Stanford University. Although it appears that much of the resentment of president and regents against Dr. Richardson was in consequence of his presidency over the Nevada chapter of the American Association of University Professors, the national officers of that body proceeded with extreme caution, and began to take a hand only when it appeared that members of the Board of Regents might attempt to imply that Dr. Richardson and the other professors involved were Communists, or at least fellow-travellers. (This insinuation was completely groundless.) Public protest against the episode was less than that sometimes stirred up in connection with political controversies inside universities, even though accounts of the affair were printed in *Time* (which referred to the amazing interrogation by President Stout as "the right to be a buttinsky"), *Newsweek*, the New York *Times*, the San Francisco *Chronicle*, and the Chicago *Tribune*—which last paper continued to take an intelligent interest in later developments in the case. This was the most callous and indefensible violation of academic freedom that has been allowed to see the light of day these many years; yet at this writing the power of President Stout and the Regents remains little shaken. Dr. Stout promptly turned to a new project of his: the establishment of a new University of Nevada, Southern Branch, to be situated at Las Vegas—for which the state of Nevada had no funds available, and for which there appeared to be no pressing need. Amplitude, for educators of Mr. Stout's persuasion, is all.

Nor did President Stout learn discretion in his relations with professors. In the autumn of 1953, he insisted that all members of the faculty subscribe to a loyalty-oath specifying that they had no Communist affiliations or associations, for the sake of "better public relations"; and two members of the faculty who protested against this indignity, though they signed, were not re-employed when their contracts expired. Upon this, an instructor in economics, Mr. Arthur L. Grey, Jr., resigned in protest against both this affair and Dr. Richardson's. "At the time," Mr. Grey said, "I did not happen to agree with Dr. Richardson's particular views on this subject, but I became gravely disturbed when I realized the administration meant to deprive him and other faculty members of their positions because of their independence of position. . . . The philosophy that the end justifies the means does not appear to me to have any place in the university. The president of Columbia University recently declared that 'Wisdom comes through knowledge, but only if knowledge has led the student to gain a set of moral and ethical principles which he can use as a chart for life.' If the university fails to give place to ethics in the governance of its own affairs, then what place do ideals have in the curriculum?" (Mr. Grey's letter of resignation, as quoted in the Reno *Evening Gazette,* May 25, 1954).

Before Mr. Grey resigned, however, the Supreme Court of Nevada had come to its decision in the case of Dr. Frank Richardson. The Court, of course, was not concerned with questions of "education for democracy" or the absolute right of the doctor of education to browbeat a mere scientist. The Court was concerned with whether sufficient legal cause was shown by the Board of Regents for the dismissal of Dr. Richardson, under the regular tenure-policies of that Board. And the Court decided, on April 23, 1954, that the Regents had not shown sufficient cause, and so ordered that Dr. Richardson be restored to his post. Professor Richardson returned to the University of Nevada in September, 1954, and resumed his duties there. Whether he will manage or desire to remain there, with the enmity of President Stout to contend against, is yet to be seen. He was vindicated thanks to the rule of law, and not by any effort of his colleagues, or of professional associations and learned societies, or because of public protest. The courts, when all is said, remain the chief defense of academic freedom when a right to tenure of an appointment can be proved. But not many professors have the resolution of Dr. Frank Richardson.

At Reno, it was clear that the very idea of justice was forgotten by the administrators of the University, who were governed by arbitrary temper and self-interest: "justice", for such persons, is simply immediate expediency. Until there is some apprehension once more, on American campuses, of what the word "justice" means, probably it will do little good to appoint committees on academic freedom and standards, for at bottom what the colleges are ailing from is a neglect of ethical principle. Until there is some return to ethical knowledge, "education" at many colleges and universities will continue to be no more than indoctrination of masses of students or a contrivance for paying salaries to administrators and professors.

Anything which encourages growth of enrollments must be good, in the opinion of the educational levellers; and if a man dissents, let him be anathema. Mr. Gilbert Highet remarks that many teachers at the great state universities and colleges often feel as if they were so many captives of a barbarian host, merely tolerated, at best, by administrators and students, as a façade for the great expensive hypocrisy called "higher education" nowadays. After all, larger enrollments may bring larger salaries and occasional promotions and more instructors under an administrator's thumb. Some nights, possibly, doubts may assail such an administrator; he may have been struck briefly by the abysmal ignorance of some confused and unhappy student; and a headache may remind him

71

that conscience, even though the vestige of a human existence less sophisticated, still cannot be amputated as if it were a vermiform appendix. Yet doubtless the wardens at the Siberian prison-camps suffer an uneasy night occasionally, too, and rise the next morning cheerfully enough, to do what is called the popular will. After all, none of us has much difficulty in remembering that he has emoluments to receive, or in forgetting that he has duties to perform; and "academic freedom" may be safely shrugged away as something one writes about for a learned journal, but which cannot possibly apply to one's own situation. And is not the Wave of the Future on the side of the big dormitories? And will we not have a great many more unsuspecting young people to be processed through our plant by 1960? And twice as many by 1970? And Lord knows how many by 1984?

III

Words without Thoughts

Now that I have shown how some of the people most fond of using the words "democracy" and "freedom" and "progress" and "education for all" are to be found in the ranks of the enemies of academic freedom, let me add that I have no intention of declaring that all disciples of John Dewey, or all pragmatists, or all professors of education, fall into this category. Some, like Professor Hook, are among the most vigorous defenders of true liberty of expression in the Academy. Nor do I hold that all persons philosophically opposed to the opinions of Dewey, or all champions of traditional society and education, or all professors of the liberal arts, are sincerely devoted to academic freedom. No philosophical system can guarantee the virtue of its disciples. "The practice of men runs not an equal pace," old Sir Thomas Browne tells us, "yea, and often runs counter to their theory; we naturally know what is good, but naturally pursue what is evil: the rhetorick wherewith I persuade another cannot persuade myself. There is a depraved appetite in us that will with patience hear the learned instructions of reason, but yet perform no further than agrees to its own irregular humour."

What I have endeavored to do in the preceding chapter is to suggest how a philosophy and an educational scheme—pragmatism and progressive education—commencing as inno-

73

vations and challenges to things established, may harden into secular dogmas; and how the second or third generation of disciples to this philosophy and this scheme of education may become smug and intolerant of any dissent, once their ideas, in the beginning heretical, have become the new orthodoxy. I think also that deep in the system of John Dewey, with its abstract and ill-defined notion of "democracy", lies an ominous tendency to suppress everything that does not conform to these vague canons of "democracy" and "progress". I shall touch on these matters again. In the present chapter, however, I am concerned chiefly with the failure of persons who are *not* pragmatic or dedicated to the education scheme of Dewey to sustain the idea of academic freedom as they should. As among the pragmatists and progressivists, so among the conservatives and scholastics of education there are men who talk a great deal concerning academic freedom, but fail to give reality to their words. Words without thoughts to Heaven never go.

Mr. Robert Hutchins has been one of the most energetic writers on academic freedom; and although I believe that some of his remarks have been silly or exaggerated, nevertheless many of his observations have been sound and true. I am an admirer of Mr. Hutchins. This is not to say that I am his disciple: for with much in his educational theories I disagree profoundly, and although there is perhaps even more in his writings and career with which I agree, still my convictions and his, even when they coincide, usually are arrived at by different chains of reasoning and are derived from different intellectual traditions. Mr. Hutchins, despite his fondness for Scholastic philosophy, is substantially in the line of eighteenth-century rationalism; while I, so far as my views are worthy to be compared with the more important views of Mr. Hutchins, am in the line of English thinkers like Elyot and Hooker and Burke, and of American thinkers like P. E. More and Irving Babbitt. But whatever disagreements I may have with Mr. Hutchins, I am convinced that he has been a great force for good in the educational system of the United States. Into a university world sinking soddenly into vocationalism, frivolity, false specialization, and the second-hand doctrines of Dewey, Hutchins brought fresh vigor and a manly challenge. Fearless and resourceful, he has labored mightily to free us from hypocrisy and mediocrity; and I think that something of his work will endure. Many projects he has undertaken too impetuously, and then dropped with still greater haste; he is not a consistent thinker, nor often an original one; but we needed him, and we ought to honor him for much that he has essayed.

And for a generous estimate of Mr. Robert M. Hutchins, I turn to the words of a gentleman whom—as I shall show in a little while—Mr. Hutchins has gravely injured: Mr. W. T. Couch, who writes, "I saw Mr. Hutchins as the best hope of education in America, brilliant and fearless in the pursuit of truth, large-minded, generous and just, capable of descending from the clouds in which university presidents too often seem to dwell and entering the battle to maintain the conditions that are necessary to decent life among human beings on this earth."

I have said that some of Mr. Hutchins' observations on academic freedom are not worthy of him; let me take up those first, and afterward his more important remarks which do something to improve our understanding of this subject. For an example of his tendency to exaggerate grossly the political menace to academic freedom at present, I extract a paragraph from an address he gave in 1949, "What Price Freedom?" He says that though we do not throw people into jail for differences with political dogma, we do throw them out of work:

> The result is that every public servant must try to remember every tea party his wife has gone to in the past ten years and endeavor to recall what representatives of which foreign powers she may have met on these occasions. A professor cannot take a

position on any public question without looking into the background of everybody who may be taking the same position on the same question. If he finds that any person who is taking the same position on this question has been charged with taking an unpopular position on another question, the professor had better not take any position on this question, or he may be hailed before some committee to explain himself.[1]

It is well to guard against frenzy over an alleged subversive conspiracy among teachers; but it is quite as important not to overshoot the mark and fall into a frenzy of an opposite character. It is true that Mr. Hutchins spoke these words before it became clear to many of us that, in truth, our nation has suffered a good deal from subversion these past few years. "But since then," as Miss Mary McCarthy says apropos of another academic denouncer of "thought control", in *The Groves of Academe*, "Dr. Fuchs had confessed; Mr. Hiss had been convicted; Mr. Greenglass and others . . . had been tried for atomic spying . . ." Since then, the slander of *Ordeal by Slander* has grown much less slanderous. Mr. Hutchins, however, preaches on in unaltered vein. In a picture-magazine, not long ago, he declared that after Senator McCarthy's attack on Harvard, benefactors would be afraid to give Harvard money.[2] No sooner had he spoken than the Rockefeller family gave many millions of dollars to the Harvard divinity school. But Professor Hook has smitten Mr. Hutchins hip and thigh for these excesses of zeal, and I shall not examine them in detail. I think it worthwhile, nevertheless, to quote here some remarks on the curious pretended terror of Senator McCarthy to which even Dr. Hutchins is addicted. Mr. Leslie A. Fiedler is the author:

> It can be asserted . . . that there is nothing easier in America at the moment than speaking ill of McCarthy. In academic circles, for instance, particularly in the East, it is generally the pro-McCarthy position which occasions resentment and even ostracism. . . . For intellectual respectability (and one can under-

stand "intellectual" in its broadest possible scope), it is *de rigueur* that one consider McCarthyism a major threat to liberty. I doubt that there has ever been gathered together a broader or more articulate united front than the one which opposes the behaviour of the present Chairman of the Permanent Sub-Committee on Investigations. . . .

And yet the statement made in article after article by the attackers of McCarthy, a statement repeated by commentators and re-echoed by commentators on the commentators, is that McCarthyism threatens, if it does not actually bludgeon into silence, all free criticism. From one end of the country to another rings the cry, "I am cowed! I am afraid to speak out!" and the even louder response, "Look, he is cowed! He is afraid to speak out!" In my own town, where it proved almost impossible to turn up a pro-McCarthy speaker for a recent forum, and where no library contains a copy of McCarthy's book, though Lattimore's version of his story is available, I have been told over and over that there is "something" now in the air which makes one swallow unsaid what once might have been spoken without a second thought.

One is tempted to laugh at first, to find only comedy in this constant frightened twittering back and forth among people who are in almost universal agreement. And yet . . .

And yet, Mr. Fiedler goes on to say, all this smoke is not without some fire: "There have been some reprisals against the holders of ideas unpopular with McCarthy; a handful of nervous regents have dropped instructors in a few universities and colleges; in the public school system, there has been an occasional firing . . ."[3] I repeat it is well that we should be on our guard, and so Mr. Fiedler says. Yet I think that much of what Mr. Hutchins has said of all this is little better than bombast.

It is not Mr. Hutchins' more passionate recent addresses, then, to which I refer when I say that he has done and said much in the cause of academic freedom. I mean, rather, the spirit which he displays when he says, in *The University of Utopia*, "The award of college credits at Florida State University for being a clown is as great a disservice to higher education and academic freedom as any of the carryings-on of Senator McCarthy or Congressman Velde."[4] Mr. Hutchins' view of these legislators considered, these are strong words; and they are true words. What Mr. Hutchins has done for the cause of academic freedom—and he has been doing it a great while—is to restore within the Academy, so far as lies in his power, a sense of the dignity which the liberal intellect ought to display, and to resist valiantly the notions of the educational levellers who would convert universities into equalitarian country-clubs and professors into dry-nurses. The freedom of the university, Mr. Hutchins writes, depends on the tradition within which the university operates, so that "the first step toward the performance of this duty is to exclude from the universities those activities which create confusion in regard to it." If the professor is metamorphosed into a custodian of delayed adolescents, and the order of teachers into "the Association of Adolescent-Sitters", there will be no freedom of thought, but only indoctrination of adolescents with a dull conformity to "adjustment to environment". If the Association of Adolescent-Sitters seeks security of tenure and freedom of speech, thought, and association, it is not really after academic freedom: it is only acting as a trade-union would, for the private advantage of its members. "Certainly it is only confusing if these claims are summarized under the name of academic freedom." If the American university and college continue to decline from the condition of institutions of learning to the condition of custodial institutions, catering to the pleasures and the snobbishness of young persons whose parents want them kept out of the way for a few awkward years, then academic freedom will decline proportionately:

> When you hear educators talk about how the educational system needs more money in order to do more things, you may suspect that they are not talking about education; they are talking about the extension of the custodial system.

America may require a custodial system for the young. If it does, that system should be called by its right name and should be appraised in the right terms. We should not try to apply educational standards to something that does not pretend to be educational. But I would point out that, if through the process of underspecialization the American educational system becomes custodial, America will then be without an educational system. Such a country is without any means for the intellectual development of its population. If the family and the church undertake this responsibility, they will in their turn become underspecialized institutions. They will fail in the educational task and also in the tasks proper to them. A country that makes no effective provision for the intellectual development of its population is headed for dictatorship or worse. A country that makes no provision for serious higher learning, such as the University of Utopia provides, will suffer from the degradation of its culture, the confusion of its thinkers, and the ultimate cessation of its scientific progress.[5]

When Mr. Hutchins writes thus, I wish fervently that he were Chancellor Hutchins again, or President Hutchins, back contending against our educational sea of troubles, instead of performing his rather nebulous duties with the rather nebulous Fund for the Republic. For Mr. Hutchins knows that if professors sink into the condition of base mechanicals, they will deserve no especial freedom. "By what stretch of the dictionary," writes to me a college president whom I esteem more than I do Mr. Hutchins, "is the technique of adding machines subsumed under the cool shadow of the grove?" The scholar and the teacher deserve their high freedom because they are professors of the true arts and sciences—that is, because their disciplines are the fields of knowledge in which there ought always to be controversy and exploration; and their especial freedom of expression and speculation is their right only while they still argue and investigate. But if this body of learned men is trampled down by a multitude of technicians, adolescent-sitters, administrators, pedagogy-specialists, and art-of-camp-cookery teachers (whose skills, however convenient to us, do not require a special freedom of mind for their conservation and growth), given the titles and emoluments of professors, then the whole order of scholars will sink into disrepute and discouragement. Or if this body of learned men, instead of being given the opportunity to teach young people who want to learn, is compelled to cajole a mob of "students" who have not the faintest inclination for books or discourse, but have come up to college just for the ride and the degree and the opportunity to bully a professor, then the scholar will flee from the Academy and its "freedom" as if from the galleys, abandoning our custodial institutions to the technicians and the adding-machine operators. "A man of ideas once said in my presence," Irving Babbitt remarks, "that intellect will tell in the long run—even in a college faculty. In the meantime he himself resigned a college position and took up another occupation in the evident fear that otherwise he might suffer the fate of Dryden's Achitophel:—

> 'Yet still he saw his fortune at a stay—
> Whole droves of blockheads choking up his way.'"

Now Mr. Hutchins never has allowed any blockheads to choke up *his* way, and he has protested manfully against our institutions of learning being choked with professors who profess nothing, and students who study nothing. I have suggested in the preceding chapter the monstrous growth of most of our universities and colleges, so that personality withers in their collectivism, and the grove of Academe becomes the asphalt jungle. Many scholars feel choked in this ant-hill system, and so do many students, or people who would like to be students, if only the college administrators would let them escape for a few hours from this babbling multitude. "How often," inquires President Gideonse of Brooklyn College, "do we successfully teach our students the essentially humanistic distinction between privacy and loneliness? Why did the solitude of Abraham Lincoln's youth lead to an outcome that differs so sharply from the 'peer group psychology' of the 'lonely crowd'?"[6]

Against the mass-man as master of the grove of Academe, Mr. Robert Hutchins has stood up with remarkable fortitude. At one time, he made an endeavor to divert the torrent of would-be college graduates into new junior colleges, in their own communities; but this has not succeeded. In 1900, there were 238,000 students in American colleges; fifty years later, there were 2,659,000. The number of bachelor's degrees awarded in 1950 was fifteen times that of 1900; the number of master's degrees was thirty-seven times that of 1900; the number of doctor's degrees, seventeen times that of 1900. Even when the increase in the American population is taken into account, this proliferation of degrees is astonishing. A great many people rejoice in it; I think, with Mr. Hutchins, and Mr. Charles Seymour, that there is much to dread in it. President McDonald of Bowling Green State University, one of the rejoicers (for has not this movement created his own institution?), suggests some consequences:

> Slowly but inevitably the classics receded into the background. Philosophy lost its dominant position and the humanities generally slipped backward relatively. Mathematics suffered heavily at first, but the emergence of the natural sciences brought a renewed and vigorous interest in this field at mid-century. Accounting, social work, textiles, journalism, ceramics—these are but a few of the hundreds of newer subjects steadily crowding out ancient subjects which even in 1900 were being viewed in nostalgia more than in practice.[7]

Just what measure of intellectual freedom either prescriptive right or modern society will guarantee to the teacher of ceramics or of weaving, I think I know. Yet this vast alteration in quantity and kind of schooling (this is not, as Mr. Hutchins says, true education) will be as nothing by the side of what the evangels of quantitative progress predict for the next decade or two. We are told that there will be an increase in application for college admission of fifty per cent by 1960; that the number of college instructors must be increased by that per cent, accordingly; and that, within that brief period, twenty-five per cent of our private colleges will go down to dusty dead. Behold Behemoth.[8] And I think, with Mr. Hutchins, that this mob of new students, made barely literate through the triumph of John Dewey's disciples in our public-school system, will be puffed up with *hubris*, mistaking their small talents for great, and telling themselves that their little stock of private reason is worth more than all the bank and capital of the ages: for will they not be freshmen, and soon doctors? Since many will be unable to meet even the present low standards of most of our colleges, standards will be lowered still further to satisfy "the demand of the market". The Professor Richardsons will have a harder time still, and the President Stouts will wax fat. As for the Bearer of the Word, who will take the trouble to pay his stipend? No one will want the Word, or almost no one, not even the Association of Adolescent-Sitters. And academic freedom? We shall be answered in the words of Lenin: "Freedom? What for? What for?"

Truly, as Burke predicted (echoing the prophet Matthew) learning will be trampled under the hoofs of the swinish multitude—and freedom in the Academy, too. Dr. Knight describes the danger and the course of action for men who think there is Truth:

First of all, I think, we must restore the intellectual fibre of higher education, but without retreating into some dream-world of an aristocratic past. To do so we must redefine for our society the genuinely important meaning behind such a hopelessly confused phrase as "equal opportunity." Does it mean in education that each man must be like everyone else, or does it mean that within the limits of law and order each man must be his best individual self? We must insist on the second of these meanings, and support our insistence by work adequate in flexibility and toughness to the needs of the individuals who ought to go to college—not merely the most brilliant 5% but the whole group to which we should be responsible—a group which we often fail to find, and even more often fail to quicken into life. We must, in short, reach the right people and reach them *effectively;* if we fail we shall be destroyed by our own creation, by our own vaunted system of mass college education whose half-trained graduates feel that they know what education is and don't really think very much of it.[9]

Mr. Robert Hutchins does know what education is, and he thinks a great deal of it. I repeat that I admire him; and if I cry "Ichabod" upon him, in my priggish way, it is because he has been, more than once, a Bearer of the Word, and may be so again. It is with much reluctance, then, that I discuss in the following section the contrast of Mr. Hutchins' practice of academic freedom, in one important instance, with his preaching of it. He has done so much to sustain the idea that it is a truly great pity to see him fall below his own standard; but it is also a lesson in Pride. What I am about to discuss here is Mr. Hutchins' removal of Mr. W. T. Couch as director of the University of Chicago Press, a business nearly as dismaying as the treatment of Professor Richardson at a very different university. Mr. Hutchins has long stood for an elevated freedom of the Academy, and so has Mr. Couch; and Mr. Couch describes this freedom better than Mr. Hutchins does:

All freedom depends on the willingness of at least some men to follow the example of Socrates. Most men are not willing to do this, and this is the basis in human experience for the ancient doctrine that all men can be divided into two classes, those who are by nature free, and those who are by nature slaves. The slave is the man whose life is governed by fear and appetite. In the modern world, the effort is made by society at times to remove fear from those who follow the calling of the teacher by saying to them: do your job honestly as teacher; offend us if you have to in order to help us learn; we will maintain you in your high calling; we will not penalize you.

2

A university press has responsibilities and rights superior to those of a commercial publishing firm. Like the university as a whole, the press enjoys a privileged status because it is dedicated not to financial profit, but to the conservation and pursuit of the truth. A press may or may not make money for its university; most such presses do not, and are subsidized heavily by their university; but even a financially sound press is intended primarily to publish books of a serious nature which might not otherwise be published, either because it would be difficult for a commercial publisher to avoid loss, or because they express truths which a commercial publisher might find it inexpedient to utter. This is a high duty, and the university press ought to enjoy a corresponding freedom of policy—governed always, of course, by a grave sense of responsibility toward the truth. The general academic freedom which appertains to the university extends also, then, to a university press. I do not mean that academic freedom ought to be extended, in its fullest measure, to everyone employed by a university, or to every function which a university may undertake: janitors, or clerks, or publicity-agents employed by a university, though they certainly are entitled to all the rights enjoyed by the employees of any concern, do not participate in academic freedom (which, I repeat, is a special and separate freedom) because they are not professors of arts and sciences or guardians of the truth; nor if the university, for its support, invests in farms or factories or commercial undertakings, it does not follow that the persons engaged to carry out these functions become the recipients of academic freedom. A university press is another matter altogether. The press is directly engaged in the principal function of the Academy, conservation and enlargement of Truth; therefore the persons responsible for the editorial policies of such a press, the men

who choose the books to be published and who are responsible
for the freedom of that press, rightfully participate in the
privilege of academic freedom. This fact is recognized at the
chief universities of America. It was recognized by the University of Chicago, which possessed the most distinguished
and successful press in the country late in the 1940's, so that
the director of the press held the rank of full professor and was
guaranteed tenure of his position as fully as any other professor. In some respects, indeed, the freedom of the university
press is *more* important than the freedom of any single professor in the university: for while a single professor has but
one voice, the university press constitutes a multitude of
voices; and if the liberty of the press is infringed, not merely
one scholar suffers, but many.

Late in November, 1950, I was surprised to learn that Mr.
W. T. Couch had been dismissed as director of the University
of Chicago Press. I made inquiries; I have been making inquiries ever since; and I have gone through a mass of papers
on the subject, and conversed with a good many people who
have some direct acquaintance with the affair. What follows,
then, is my considered opinion on the cause and significance
of the dismissal of Mr. Couch, which I believe to be a most
ominous blow to academic freedom.

When Mr. Couch was dismissed, on November 20, 1950, I
did not have the honor of a personal acquaintance either with
Mr. Couch or with Mr. Hutchins; but I thought of Mr. Couch
as the leading scholarly editor in America, and of Mr. Hutchins as the most forceful university president in America. For
twenty years Mr. Couch had been connected with the University of North Carolina Press, as assistant director and then
director; there he had made his mark; and Mr. Hutchins had
invited him to the University of Chicago. Like Mr. Hutchins,
Mr. Couch was fearless, resourceful, and disdainful of shams.
At Chicago, Mr. Couch employed his remarkable talents as
editor and administrator and man of ideas to make the Press

both the most lively and the most profitable undertaking of the sort in the whole country. At the time of his dismissal, the Press enjoyed a larger volume of business than any other, and had recently published so many books of distinguished scholarship that I, like many others, thought the University of Chicago Press held leadership in its field almost without challenge. Both Mr. Hutchins and Mr. Couch, everyone knew, approved of controversy, as the life-blood of civilization; thus the Press published stimulating books, as well as scholarly books. I had always thought that Mr. Hutchins must be enormously pleased with Mr. Couch's accomplishment. However could he have made up his mind to discharge the man he himself had invited to the University?

At first, no one could offer me any but the vaguest explanations; then I was informed that the University had dismissed Mr. Couch (with only six and one-half hours' notice) because he had "demonstrated his inability to get along with his subordinates or superiors." This charge could have a most grave effect upon Mr. Couch's future, if people should believe it; its very imprecision might harm him more than anything else. How was it, after Mr. Couch had been at the University for five years, that the administrators of the University could come suddenly to this conclusion and find it necessary to be rid of Mr. Couch before the day was out? And this charge also seemed to have the false ring of so many similar vague reasons given for the dismissal of professors whose competence everyone had taken to be beyond reproach. I was not satisfied with this curt official explanation; and the refusal of the University's authorities to discuss the matter further with anyone made me still more desirous to look into the whole affair. Mr. Couch himself, for a time, could not understand why he had been dismissed: he had been given not the slightest warning, and no one in authority had intimated that his direction of the press was unsatisfactory.

One needs first to inquire into the official explanation. How did Mr. Couch get along with his subordinates? During his directorship, the turn-over of employees, previously excessive, had been sharply reduced. The personnel manager of the Press stated, two days after his dismissal, that he knew of not a single employee, at any time, who had been discharged because of difficulties with Mr. Couch. And after Mr. Couch was discharged, the associate editor, the editorial assistant, the syllabi editor, the assistant to the production editor, the sales manager, the assistant to the sales manager, and the trade sales manager resigned in protest against this action. I think it unlikely that any other editor in the country could have commanded such loyalty among his subordinates. These are not the marks of a man who is unable to get along with his subordinates. Indeed, the evidence was so overwhelming that Mr. Couch was a popular administrator that the University presently withdrew this charge, saying only that he had not been able to get along with his superiors.

Now just how did Mr. Couch get along with his superiors? Mr. Couch had two sets of superiors, scholarly and administrative. His scholarly superiors, the members of the Board of University Publications which supervises the performance of the Press, do not seem to have felt that Mr. Couch was a difficult subordinate. On the contrary, on November 22 fifteen present and former members of this board, scholars of professorial rank, addressed an open letter to him in which they expressed their confidence in the most vigorous terms:

We desire to tell you at once that we are deeply shocked to receive your letter of yesterday, addressed to present members of the Board of University Publications, or to learn in other ways that you have been summarily dismissed. . . . In particular, we are astounded at the reasons given—inability to get along with your subordinates or superiors. We have not found you hard to get along with, in any sense, but an esteemed colleague, coworker and friend. We do recognize that you have persisted in standing for the integrity of scholarly publication in a way which might well arouse opposition. But we think this is a virtue, not a fault . . .

These scholarly superiors had not even been consulted by the administrators who dismissed Mr. Couch.

The administrative superiors of Mr. Couch were the chancellor of the University (then Mr. Hutchins), its president (then Mr. Colwell), and its vice-president in charge of business affairs (then Mr. J. A. Cunningham). Had Mr. Couch been insubordinate toward these gentlemen? A faculty committee which was formed to investigate this dismissal, and which we may call the Hodges Committee, wrote in its report: "We who have had access to the documents and testimony bearing on the case know that there has been no slightest suggestion of misconduct. . . . No hearings were held prior to the dismissal nor did Mr. Couch have any opportunity to defend himself on charges of inadequate performance of duties." And a letter addressed to the university administration on November 23, signed by seven members of the Publications Board, said, "We all believe that he has done a distinguished job as Editor, and that he has administered the editorial affairs of the Press in accordance with the best academic traditions of the University of Chicago." Here is no suggestion of misconduct, or of incompetence, or of mismanagement. A firm of management consultants had then just completed a study of the operation of the Press and had pronounced it sound. There had been no hearings and no reprimands. Surely, if Mr. Couch had been difficult to get along with, his administrative superiors had made no such complaint to him or to anyone else, and there was no outward sign that this alleged insubordination had adversely influenced the Press.

Now these facts tend to suggest that the official apology— that Mr. Couch could not get along with subordinates or superiors—does not explain the dismissal nor the sudden manner in which it was executed. I believe that we must look elsewhere for the real causes. The Chicago *Tribune* (November 22, 1950), whose representative had asked the vice-president of the University what had happened at the Press, quoted that gentleman as answering that "the matter is private." It was hardly a satisfactory reply. When the director of a leading scholarly press is dismissed in an abrupt manner, the event is of concern to everyone who values academic freedom. On November 29, the American Association of University Presses respectfully asked the Chancellor and the Board of Trustees for some fuller explanation; that letter never was answered or even acknowledged, until well after Mr. Hutchins, Mr. Colwell, and Mr. Cunningham all three had left the University of Chicago. At last, upon being asked again by the Association of University Presses, the new Chancellor, Mr. Kimpton, two years later, acknowledged the inquiry and said only that "Mr. Couch was dismissed because he and his superiors were unable to work harmoniously together." (This would have been quite as true, and as insufficient, an explanation of the dismissal of Professor Richardson at the University of Nevada.) Mr. Kimpton, apparently somewhat embarrassed at the whole affair, in which he had played no part but which had been bequeathed to him by his predecessor in office, prefaced this laconic explanation with the remark, "Moreover, we do not feel that a principle of academic freedom is involved in this case." Perhaps it is worth remarking here, parenthetically, that I never have found a single case of disagreement over academic freedom in which the administrators of a college or university would confess that the principle was involved at all. Everyone cherishes academic freedom—in the abstract.

"Arbitrary action by the administration of the University of Chicago, world famous for its advocacy of academic freedom," the letter of the Association of University Presses to Chancellor Hutchins and the Trustees had said, "will be a blow to intellectual freedom everywhere." And so it has been.

But our search for the true cause of Mr. Couch's dismissal is assisted by the following statement contained in the report of the Hodges Committee: "Two years earlier, Mr. Couch had been in open conflict with senior officers of the administration preceding the publication of Grodzins' *Americans Betrayed*. According to statements made to the [committee] the administration at about this time wished to discontinue Mr. Couch's services."

Mr. Couch was not unaccustomed to "open conflict" with administrative officers. During his years at the University of North Carolina Press, he had often engaged in protracted and intense arguments with the president of that university, Mr. Frank Graham, a gentleman quite as noted for vigor of character and championship of liberal causes as Mr. Robert M. Hutchins. When Mr. Couch began his work at North Carolina, in 1925, he had been told that the press there would destroy itself if anything was published which dealt seriously with race, religion, or economics. But Mr. Couch had published a great many books at North Carolina on such subjects, because he thought that they were good books, and that such subjects ought to be discussed in the South, as elsewhere. His debates with Mr. Graham, however serious, never had caused any personal animosity; and Mr. Couch's policies had vastly increased the reputation and strength of the University of North Carolina Press, instead of destroying it. On coming to Chicago, Mr. Couch had assumed that he would be not only permitted, but expected, to exercise the same frankness and the same resolution there. But he seems to have reckoned without his man.

After examining all the evidence available to me, I have come to the conclusion that Mr. Couch was dismissed by Mr. Hutchins because he published Mr. Morton Grodzins' book *Americans Betrayed,* and for no other substantial reason. It has been suggested to me that Mr. Hutchins may have resented the publication of certain other books which Mr. Couch chose to make available. Certainly some books which the University of Chicago Press brought out during the period of Mr. Couch's directorship caused criticism of the University and of its Chancellor; it would have been a poor press, unworthy of its name, if it had not published some books vigorous enough, on important subjects, to awaken controversy. There was, for instance, Mr. Richard Weaver's book *Ideas Have Consequences*, a powerful and learned attack on relativism and positivism, which was bitterly attacked by certain reviewers noted for their doctrinaire liberalism, like the late Dixon Wecter, who had not hesitated to denounce Mr. Hutchins, as well as Mr. Weaver, for being so presumptuous as to dare to express conservative views. Now Mr. Hutchins has long been peculiarly sensitive to criticism from "liberals", and has endeavored to convince them that, though perhaps educationally conservative, he is politically liberal. But when Mr. Couch sent him a copy of *Ideas Have Consequences*, Mr. Hutchins' only comment was, "I am much impressed." If he had any objection to the book, he never said so, and so one must presume that he did not hold its publication against Mr. Couch. Another book attacked in some quarters was Mr. Frank Reel's *The Trial of General Yamashita*, which described the arbitrary trial and execution of a Japanese general made a scapegoat during the early months of General MacArthur's occupation of Japan. Here, again, Mr. Hutchins made no complaint. Mr. Robert Hutchins never was a man to dread controversy, and I think it would be unfair to him to maintain that he was alarmed at Mr. Couch's boldness.

Now Mr. Morton Grodzins' *Americans Betrayed* was a book of the sort which, ordinarily, Chancellor Hutchins would have approved. It dealt with the injustice of herding a multitude of Japanese-Americans into concentration-camps during the war, with only the flimsiest of pretexts that there might be traitors among them. This was one of the most shameful episodes in the history of the United States; Mr. Grodzins' book was competently written and thoroughly documented; it deserved to be published. There is no reason to suppose that Mr. Hutchins disagreed with the thesis of *Americans Betrayed*. What seems to have angered Mr. Hutchins is that, for other reasons (and those insufficient reasons, in my judgment), he had made up his mind that the book should not be published; but that Mr. Couch had insisted on publishing it, after all. With too many of us, principle goes out the window when self-esteem is brought into question; but a distinguished educator and champion of academic freedom has obligations of which most of us are free.

The manuscript of *Americans Betrayed* had been accepted for publication by the Publications Board of the University of Chicago in July, 1948; and the Press was about to publish the book when a foundation connected with the University of California sent a letter to the University of Chicago Press protesting against publication. The author, these persons said, who formerly had been at California and was then at the University of Chicago, was guilty of literary piracy, shoddy scholarship, and breach of trust; they further asserted that Mr. Grodzins had agreed in writing not to publish his work. In later correspondence, the officers of this foundation withdrew their assertion that the author had entered into such an agreement, and alleged simply that he had no lawful right to publish the product of his research because at the time he had undertaken the work he had held only a position of minor importance at the University of California.

The issue, clearly, was a legal one. Mr. Couch referred the question to the legal counsel of the university; and that counsel agreed with the assertion of the foundation at the University of California. Mr. Couch appealed to the president of the University of Chicago, and the president, too, agreed with California's position. Then Mr. Couch consulted two leading members of the university's law school. These scholars agreed with Mr. Couch that the laws of literary property gave Mr.

Grodzins the right to publish his manuscript as he might choose. Because of this disagreement, Mr. Couch then proposed to clarify the matter by seeking the advice of a specialist on literary property and its rights, outside the university. But the university administration forbade Mr. Couch, in writing, to arrange for this opinion.

The principal objection of the university administrators to the publication of *Americans Betrayed* seems to have been their feeling that it would disturb what they called "inter-university comity". Now this phrase surely is not Mr. Hutchins'; he never employs the jargon of the educational bureaucrat. And perhaps the idea was not originally Mr. Hutchins', either, for he never has been conspicuously zealous for inter-university comity, and only shortly before this had been most active in assailing the administration of the University of California for its insistence that professors there take an oath of loyalty; indeed, he had proposed that all scholars contribute from their salaries to make up a fund for the maintenance of the non-jurors at California. It is possible, and even probable, that Mr. Hutchins' decision that *Americans Betrayed* should not be published was taken simply in hasty support of his subordinates; and, having once decided, Mr. Hutchins was too proud to turn back.

Mr. Couch discussed the matter thoroughly with Mr. Colwell and Mr. Hutchins, separately. Mr. Colwell, apparently speaking for himself and the Chancellor, said he could not understand why Mr. Couch took such an interest in the matter. Mr. Grodzins, the President stated, was only fighting for power, and cared nothing for principle; his only thought was for advancement, by whatever means and at anyone's expense. "I did not either trust or distrust Grodzins," Mr. Couch writes. "I simply suspended judgment on him and worked to maintain what I considered decent standards in scholarly publishing. I told Colwell I couldn't shape my attitude toward manuscripts by considerations of whether or not their authors were concerned only with getting power for themselves." Mr. Couch maintained that the real issues were these: whether a university press should suppress a book simply at the arbitrary request of another university; whether a university press and a great university should allow an author's reputation to be seriously—perhaps irreparably—damaged by such an act, which would imply that the press and the university agreed that he had stolen or misused the materials for his book; whether the laws of literary property should be set aside, and the rights of authors and the public disregarded, merely for the sake of "inter-university comity".

President Colwell stood by his decision: if California would not give permission that the book be published, it must be dropped. Mr. Couch appealed to Chancellor Hutchins. The Chancellor took the matter out of Mr. Couch's hands, informing him that he, the Chancellor, would handle the matter himself in discussion with officials at California. This was the state of affairs which Mr. Couch reported to the Publications Board in October, and again in November, 1948.

It cannot be held that the university administration was quite unaware that the rights of the author were involved. The minutes of the November meeting of the Publications Board are sufficiently clear on this point: "Mr. Colwell stated that the Central Administration considered the case very serious and had intervened because it felt that all rights in the case ought to be respected, whether they were the rights of California or of the author." Why, then, the written order to Mr. Couch preventing him from determining exactly what were the rights in the case? The answer is that legal considerations were not the only considerations involved; for, as the same minutes record, "Mr. Colwell said the matter involved the relationship of Chicago with another University, and this in turn raised the issue who had final authority on questions of this kind."

Now I am inclined to think that if a dispute between two universities turns on a question of law, the authority to deter-

94

mine the issue is the law of the land, ascertainable through qualified legal counsel. The administration of the University of Chicago was of another mind. According to the minutes, "Mr. Colwell said the Director [Mr. Couch] had taken the position that Mr. Hutchins did not have the authority to make a final decision." And Chancellor Hutchins "had stated flatly that the case did not involve freedom of opinion." A mad world, my masters. In the Chancellor's opinion, apparently, no question was involved except whether the University of Chicago should risk the displeasure of the University of California. The argument expounded by the university administration, then, ran thus: since inter-university relations were involved, the Chancellor alone had the right to make a final decision. While the rights of both parties had to be considered, it was not advisable to determine precisely what these rights were. The question of freedom of opinion was not involved.

The stand of Mr. Couch was this: the rights of both parties ought to be taken seriously, and the law should be consulted to determine exactly what these rights were. If California's protest was justified, the book should be dropped. If California's protest was not justified, the book should be published. But to drop the book merely because of California's desires, not backed by rights, would constitute a suppression of the book by the University of Chicago, a violation of the principle of freedom of opinion and of the freedom that a great university ought to extend to scholars.

These arguments, obviously, are in open conflict. Mr. Couch was thoroughly aroused by the possibility that the Chancellor might make the decision which his remark, reported above, seemed to foreshadow. He did not hide his alarm, knowing that once the Chancellor had announced his decision, it would be binding on the director of the Press. The minutes of the Board of Publications confirm this:

He [Mr. Couch] said that while he did not and could not question Mr. Hutchins' authority in the matter, he felt he was entitled

to know the facts and principles and he felt the Board was entitled to know the facts and principles on the basis of which any
decision was made. In the Director's opinion, the suppression of
a manuscript and freedom of opinion were involved. In matters
of such primary importance it is necessary that everyone understand clearly where the University stands.

Mr. Couch also discussed the matter in detail with individual
members of the Publications Board, and with a number of
other faculty members. Several shared his alarm. The result
was that the university administration found itself in the position that it could not forbid publication of *Americans Betrayed* without having to give reasons for its decision—reasons
which must satisfy a number of influential members of the
faculty.

And so, at length, *Americans Betrayed* was published, even
though the California foundation did not withdraw its objections. But Mr. Couch had done what his fifteen scholarly superiors recalled at the time of his dismissal: he had "persisted in
standing for the integrity of scholarly publication." In a matter of principle, he had challenged authority in the university
—"which might well arouse opposition." It is a matter of record that Mr. Couch's stand for freedom of expression here *did*
arouse the opposition of the university administrators. It
seems to me certain that Mr. Couch was dismissed, two years
later, because of this stand he made.

There is more evidence than that given above. For instance,
Mr. Fred Wieck, the associate editor of the Press, had a conference of two and a half hours, on November 19, 1950, with
President Colwell; this was the Sunday just preceding the dismissal of Mr. Couch. The tenor of Mr. Colwell's remarks on
that occasion convinced Mr. Wieck that Mr. Hutchins had
not forgiven Mr. Couch for his opposition, and that Mr. Colwell, whether he liked it or not, was saddled with the responsibility of settling scores. Mr. Wieck states that President Colwell told him "that Mr. Hutchins and he had made up their

minds some time back, that they had told Mr. Cunningham when Cunningham first joined the University that he should get rid of Couch. Mr. Colwell then brought up the Grodzins affair. . . . This affair is the key to the whole thing."

It was Mr. Cunningham, Vice-President in charge of Business Affairs, who notified Mr. Couch personally of his dismissal. At that time, Mr. Couch learned, in reply to his astounded inquiry as to the reason for this abrupt dismissal, that "I had shown myself completely incapable of getting along with my superiors and my subordinates." And, besides, Mr. Cunningham went on to say, when he himself first came to the University, Mr. Hutchins and Mr. Colwell had told him to get rid of Couch. Now Mr. Cunningham came to the University of Chicago in November, 1948, during the heat of the discussion over *Americans Betrayed*. Vice-President Cunningham made these statements to others besides Mr. Couch; but he refused to write down for Mr. Couch these charges against him. Mr. Cunningham suggested to Mr. Wieck and others, immediately after the dismissal, that they doubtless would meet with inquiries about the matter, but that they had best "not talk about it—just pass all inquiries on to me; just turn the heat on me." He told members of the Hodges Committee, who had hoped that he would suspend the dismissal pending their investigation, that regardless of their Committee's findings "the eventual outcome would have been the same."

Seven professors of the university stated that they were "perturbed" and "embarrassed" by the manner of Mr. Couch's ouster. Fifteen spoke of being "shocked", and of a "wrong done" Mr. Couch. The Hodges Committee reported "a gross violation of rights" and "violation of tenure". None of them received the courtesy of an answer from the university administration. Inquiries of one sort or another were undertaken by the Association of American University Presses and by the American Civil Liberties Union; they began with some zeal, but the University of Chicago answered principally with silence, and presently, as many such investigations do, the inquiries dwindled away to nothing. The kindest description of these attempts is "feeble". The Hodges Committee accepted Mr. Couch's dismissal as a thing done and not to be undone, and so presently fell silent. Mr. Couch left the field of university publishing in disgust. Despite the courage and loyalty of some individuals among his colleagues, in general anyone who reviews the case must be reminded of John Jay Chapman's description of pusillanimity in college faculties:

> The average professor in an American college will look on at an act of injustice done to a brother professor by their college president with the same unconcern as the rabbit who is not attacked watches the ferret pursue his brother up and down through the warren to predestinate and horrible death. We know, of course, that it would cost the non-attacked rabbit his place to express sympathy for the martyr; and the non-attacked is poor, and has offspring, and hope of advancement. The non-attacked rabbit would, of course, become a suspect, and a marked man the moment he lifted up his voice in defense of rabbit-rights. I am not, however, here raising the question of general ethics; I refer to the philosophical belief, to the special theory of *professional* ethics which forbids a professor to protect his colleague. . . . The public must be appealed to by the professor himself in all ways and upon all occasions. The professor must teach the nation to respect learning; he must make the nation understand the function and the rights of the learned classes. He must do this through a willingness to speak and to fight for himself.

Mr. Couch possesses that willingness to speak and to fight for himself, and so does Mr. Hutchins. What Mr. Hutchins lacks is the tolerance of that quality in others: confronted by a man as resolute, intelligent, and ready to stand by principle as himself, he abandoned his own championship of academic freedom, forgot the honor of his own university, violated his own tenure-policies, and forced out of university publishing the ablest man in the whole field—all for the sake of gratifying a wounded ego. Words without thoughts, I repeat, never to

Heaven go. Doubtless the members of the faculty at the University of Chicago were prudent in not protesting with undue vehemence against the dismissal of a colleague: for Mr. Hutchins forgets nothing. I still hope, however, that he, unlike Louis XVIII, admits the possibility of learning something.

I do not mean to leave the reader with a nasty taste in his mouth, though: this story has a happy ending. President Colwell, not long after his somewhat indiscreet remark that the decision to discharge Mr. Couch had been agreed upon after the Grodzins affair, found himself no longer president of the University of Chicago, but translated to a deanship at a university in Georgia. Vice-President Cunningham, too, has vanished from Chicago. And everyone knows what has been the reward of Mr. Hutchins: having settled scores with Mr. Couch, he promptly accepted a vice-presidency in the Ford Foundation and made his way to the sunshine of Pasadena, where he is now president of the Fund for the Republic, an offshoot of the Ford Foundation. This Fund for the Republic is dedicated to the preservation of liberty in America. Mr. Hutchins, having said and written a great deal about liberty, particularly academic liberty, makes an ideal president.

And what of Mr. Grodzins? Mr. Morton Grodzins, concerning whose motives and integrity Mr. Hutchins and Mr. Colwell expressed such unverifiable doubts? Mr. Morton Grodzins, author of *Americans Betrayed*, for whom Mr. W. T. Couch sacrificed his career? Why, a year after the dismissal of Mr. Couch, the University of Chicago was looking for a new director of their Press, which had suffered somewhat from the departure of Mr. Couch. The new chancellor of the university —let us think that he was doing his best to spread oil on troubled waters—offered this post to Mr. Grodzins, who accepted it with alacrity. Whatever his conduct toward his subordinates, Mr. Grodzins appears to have demonstrated his ability to get along with his superiors, and to avoid open conflicts, or even closed conflicts: for presently he was elevated to the deanship of the social sciences at the university. It is all very much like a fable by George Ade.

3

"Academic freedom will be preserved," an editorial writer for the Chicago *Tribune* stated nearly ten years ago, "when men who have the power to discipline professors deliberately refrain from doing so in the belief that the search for truth should be unhampered." Most writers and speakers on academic freedom pay a great deal of attention to the problem of persuading trustees and politicians and alumni and the general public to tolerate the debates and even the excesses of the Academy; but they do not say half enough about the pressing necessity for persuading presidents to tolerate professors, and professors to tolerate one another. Chancellor Hutchins said that no disregard of intellectual freedom was involved in the contemplated suppression of *Americans Betrayed;* Chancellor Kimpton said that no violation of academic freedom was involved in the dismissal of Mr. W. T. Couch. "Things and actions are what they are," Bishop Butler tells us, "and the consequences of them will be what they will be; why then should we desire to be deceived?" President Stout solemnly assured officers of the American Association of University Professors that since he did not accuse Professor Richardson of being a Communist, no violation of academic freedom was involved in that affair: he was simply trying to rid himself of an obdurate professor who stood in the way of his projected reforms.

A principal difference between Mr. Hutchins and Mr. Stout is this: Mr. Stout is a stupid man, and Mr. Hutchins is a brilliant one. Mr. Stout is a disgrace to American education, and Mr. Hutchins is a saviour of American education. But I do have something to say for Mr. Stout, and it is this: being stupid, he may actually believe what he says. Mr. Hutchins, not being stupid, cannot really believe that nothing he does ever violates academic freedom.

Neither Mr. Stout nor Mr. Hutchins, in this, stands alone. Almost all the current discussion of academic freedom is concerned with questions of political expression—the persecution of followers of Mr. Henry Wallace, or the rights and turpitude of Communist professors, or the activities of Senator McCarthy and Representative Velde. I do not object to ample and serious discussion of these problems; indeed, it is a pity that we do not carry on such discussion more regularly and consistently. When the late Charles A. Beard was hounded out of Columbia University during the First World War for his opinions upon American participation in that struggle, the New York *Times* rejoiced in an editorial entitled "The Deliverance of Columbia". Deliver us from such intolerance.

But now and then we ought to recall Gissing's aphorism that "politics is the preoccupation of the quarter-educated." The primary concern of the scholar, after all, is not with practical politics, but with learning in all its higher forms. The scholar does right, when he has the capacity and the opportunity, to take his part in practical politics; yet while he guards this right of his, he ought to guard still more jealously his right to unhampered discussion of the problems of education and ethics and history and natural science.

"An academic institution is an arena," says Professor Edward C. Kirkland. "Into it ride different contestants. They may uphold different causes, some perhaps wholly or partially wrong. They may be differently armed. But all must meet the test of conflict, of argument, and of performance." Then Mr. Kirkland proceeds to suggest the danger of confusing this contest with a program for political indoctrination, of whatever complexion, and to warn us against an unhealthy fascination with the higher learning as a means to obtain conformity to some ideology, which tendency may be discerned in much of the controversy over the political aspects of academic freedom:

> I am convinced that an understanding on this score is the correct answer to the growing tendency on the part of our governors and of some people to talk and act as if it were the duty of educational institutions and those in them to hew to the line of governmental policy, particularly foreign policy. Some of the evidence for this trend is innocuous and noncommittal, except by implication. A distinguished soldier, decked with the laurels of war, in his inaugural address as president of a great American university feels that universities should teach the American way of life. A commission of educational experts, the President's Commission on Higher Education, draws up objectives for American colleges and universities. Probably critics have been so busy belaboring the highly vulnerable parts of this six-volume document and publicists and pedagogues so agitated, favorably or otherwise, that few have noted, or at least commented upon, the purposes of higher education as the Commission saw it. "Education for a fuller realization of democracy in every phase of living. Education directly and explicitly for international understanding and cooperation. Education for the application of creative imagination and trained intelligence to the solution of social problems and to the administration of public affairs." While it does not say these are the only goals of higher education, apparently a good share of the instruction now given in the arts and humanities and perhaps even the enlargement of the area of pure science are either to halt or proceed at half pace since the goals I have recited for you "should come first in our time." They are narrow, and they are programmatic.*

Most of our concern for academic freedom has been too closely related to this sort of concern for ideological improve-

---

* Edward C. Kirkland, "Academic Freedom and the Community", in *Freedom and the University* (Cornell University Press, 1950), 121–24. I consider this one of the soundest essays on the subject among the many that I have read; and I am correspondingly surprised at the vehement denunciation of it by Mr. William J. Buckley, Jr., in *God and Man at Yale*. Mr. Buckley goes so far as to call Mr. Kirkland an extremist. I am so fortunate as to know a little about conservatism, in both the broader and narrower usages of that valuable word; and I feel that Professor Kirkland's remarks are truly conservative and prudent.

ment. I think that we have neglected, rather shabbily, the numerous dangers to true academic freedom which exhibit no immediate political aspects. Let me offer a few examples.

A professor of classics at a state college was invited to address a civic group in a small city more than a hundred miles from his college, upon some topic in the field of pedagogy. He consented, and addressed to his audience a moderate criticism of certain excesses of "learning by doing" and "socialization" in the public schools; he made no reference to any particular advocates of these schemes, nor to his own college. Upon his return, he was summoned to an audience with the dean of his division, who informed him that word of this talk had come to the ears of the department of education at the college, and that members of the staff of that department had protested. The dean, observing that the college was committed to support of all the policies of the department of education because thus more and more students would be attracted to the college from the high schools, severely reprimanded the professor of classics, and went so far as to inform him that he could expect no promotion thereafter, no matter what amends he might try to make. (And the professor has not since been promoted.) "You understand that this is not a question of academic freedom," the dean concluded. "It is simply a question of policy."*

An instructor in history at a small private college in New

---

* The dismaying intolerance of many professional educationists, in both the universities and the public schools, is described in Mr. Arthur Bestor's *Educational Wastelands,* Mr. Albert Lynd's *Quackery in the Public Schools,* Canon Bernard Iddings Bell's *Crisis in Education,* Mr. Mortimer Smith's *And Madly Teach* and his later *The Diminished Mind,* Mr. Gordon K. Chalmers' *The Republic and the Person,* and Mr. Harold L. Clapp's "The Stranglehold on Education", *American Association of University Professors Bulletin,* summer, 1949, 335–48. So far as I have been able to ascertain, no national or state legislator advocates any surveillance over the content and methods of teaching so severe as such educationists desire for their own educational scheme—and, indeed, already exercise to a large extent.

Jersey lectured to a class upon the character of St. Joan of Arc, offering several interpretations of her nature and mission —the view of her English enemies, the modern view of the Catholic church, the view of certain modern psychologists, the view of the French patriot, and the like. He did not himself advocate any particular view. The president of the college, having called him into his office, informed him that he had learned of this folly, and that the instructor had best seek employment elsewhere for the coming year. "The Catholic population of the surrounding communities is increasing steadily, and we can't afford to offend the families of potential students." It should be noted that this college president was not himself a Catholic, and, so far as I know, had received no protests from the Catholic clergy. But he was sedulous to *anticipate* possible and deplorable controversy.

An instructor in political science at a Middlewestern state teachers' college resigned in dismay at the positive contempt for learning or any formal discipline displayed by administration, staff, and many students. The college president, puzzled that anyone should voluntarily quit a position with a decent salary, asked the instructor for his reasons; he gave them. "Perhaps you don't understand what we are trying to do here," said the president. "We are trying to drain the swamps and clear away the forests of ignorance." The instructor replied that he thought he would prefer even the frontiers of education to the backwoods. He might have done well to have added that Dr. Faustus would be a valuable addition to the staff.

A professor of intellectual history attended a P.T.A. meeting at which a member of the staff of the state department of education boasted of the superiority of American schools over all educational systems of the past or of foreign parts, and denounced the German schools and universities because they had believed in disciplining of the mind, "which led straight to Naziism." The professor in the audience, an American citizen of foreign birth, had some direct acquaintance with several educational systems, particularly the English, though he held American university degrees; and so, when the question-period came, he ventured to rise and deny that the lecturer had accurately represented German principles of education. He was hissed and reproached by many persons in the audience; and, the next day, he was sternly reproved, and threatened with disciplinary action, by officials of his college; he had interfered with "good public relations", instead of sticking to the job he was hired to do.

A professor of history resigned from a large state college in protest against a deliberate lowering of standards, calculated to attract more students and pay for more dormitories. His action was followed by what, in all charity, one can describe only as a wave of vituperation from the zealots of aggrandizement. His remarks were called "irresponsible defamation" and "completely untrue"; he was said to entertain educational ideas a hundred years old (derived, in considerable part, from Jefferson—and this dread accusation pronounced by another professor of history); he "had got in with an aristocratic crowd" (which deserves a cartoon by Max Beerbohm); he was charged with resigning in order to publicize a recent book of his (which notion suggests that some educational administrators have a curious concept of the profits to be derived from the sale of scholarly works); he was admonished "to go lecture at some small college, and teach a handful of rich men's sons, but it is our duty to educate everyone we can. That's what the people of this state want." Across the alley from his rooms in a decayed house, as he read this last exhortation, he noticed a line of sleek convertibles, belonging to students, the proletarians whom the college was seeking to redeem. A colleague of his presented to the local chapter of the Association of University Professors a resolution censuring the college administration for using such language toward a scholar who had been a member of the staff for seven years, merely because he chose to resign. But a young instructor in political science, with hopes of advancement, raised his sweet voice to declare, "This case isn't important enough for us to discuss. Let's get back to talking about the right of Communists to teach."

I am reminded of Matthew Arnold's description of the liberals of his age, in his essay on "The Function of Criticism at the Present Time." He makes his liberals exclaim, " 'Let us have a social movement, let us organize and combine a party to pursue truth and new thought, let us call it *the liberal party*, and let us all stick to each other, and back each other up. Let us have no nonsense about independent criticism and intellectual delicacy, and the few and the many . . . we are all in the same movement, we are all liberals, we are all in pursuit of truth.' In this way the pursuit of truth becomes really a social, practical, pleasurable affair, almost requiring a chairman, a secretary, and advertisements; with the excitement of an occasional scandal . . . but, in general, plenty of bustle and very little thought. To act is so easy, as Goethe says; to think is so hard!"

In the long run, and perhaps even in the short run, the panel discussion of academic freedom will accomplish little enough to keep that idea and what is left of that reality from slipping away into Limbo. We need, more than any amount of lamentation, people like Mr. Richardson and Mr. Couch, who know what it is to be a man. Otherwise our colleges will soon be dominated, at the very best, by scholars like the worn-out English professor of history in Mr. Wyndham Lewis' *Self-Condemned*, sunk into apathy in an American university. "And the Faculty had no idea that it was a glacial shell of a man who had come to live among them, mainly because they were themselves unfilled with anything more than a little academic stuffing."

IV

The Professor in Politics

SOME FEW MONTHS ago, a former Communist agent, now employed by a federal agency to help ferret out people who are still Communist agents, stated that a certain professor of English literature at a state college had been, to his certain knowledge, a member of a Communist cell at a Southern university, during the 'thirties. The newspapers took up the matter with their accustomed eagerness. I was acquainted with this professor, who, what with his sombre nature, his grim manner, and his private tribulations, always had reminded me of Trollope's Perpetual Curate of Hogglestock; so let us call him Mr. Crawley. This Professor Crawley was a person of so unpredictable and iconoclastic a humor that I was surprised to learn he ever had been a regular member of the Communist Party; I had thought that, like Professor Mulcahy in *The Groves of Academe*, he would have hung mordantly on the outskirts of the Party, rather playing with the notion of entering its inner circle, yet restrained by his contempt for all humankind, even Communist humankind. I had thought that he would have behaved after the fashion of Mulcahy as the Proletarian Poet describes him:

"He came to a meeting or two," said Keogh. "Under my steering. He stood in the back of the hall, with arms folded, so." Keogh folded his arms, high on his heavy chest, and looked round the room, sardonically, while the company chuckled. "He asked some satirical questions. Later, he informed me that these *lumpen-*intellectuals had nothing to say to him. He was one of those birds that are more Communist than the Communists in theory, but you'll never meet them on the picket-line. A weird, isolated figure, with a talent for self-dramatization."[1]

My Professor Crawley, nevertheless, had ventured for a time into the inner sanctum, it appears. It is not really difficult for a man who detests humankind in the flesh to persuade himself that he loves humankind in the abstract. What attracted Dr. Crawley to the Party was a taste for eschatology, I suppose. A secular Jansenist, what the Irish call a "spiled praist", his face lit up with something resembling pleasure only when he talked of the rapidly-approaching Götterdämmerung of this abominable age in which he had the misfortune to exist, Professor Crawley joined the Party as, under other circumstances, he might have taken monastic vows. When I was with him, I always had to restrain an impulse to hum the *Dies Irae*. He could never have been a very good Communist; far from proselytizing successfully, he must have repelled any acolyte; and after a time he ceased to have any active part: whether he drifted away, or was elbowed out as useless, I cannot say, though I suspect the latter, for the chief of the Communist cell at that Southern university was a clever and unscrupulous departmental chairman, impelled by *pleonexia* from an innocuous socialism to the most efficient leadership of a society for subversion; and this strong-willed energumen would have perceived in a very little while the shortcomings of his new recruit. Well, he ceased to be a Party member, and went North, returning to his old religion of Pure Scholarship. Every man of us must have his god, I repeat, and Professor Crawley's god was Defecated Research. This is a better creed than many, though it does not warm the heart. He was not a good teacher, in the narrower sense of that expression: indeed, he was kicked upstairs into the graduate school because of his contempt for undergraduates; he could not abide them, nor they him. Yet he knew a good deal about medieval literature, and in that field, at least, was a servant of the truth. If he was a curmudgeon—why, a few curmudgeons do no harm at a university; they give some relief, often enough, from the insipid smile of "a friendly campus", dedicated to giving the public what it wants. Eccentricity is one of the prescriptive rights that make up academic freedom.

Professor Crawley did not abandon his peculiar version of Marxism. The events of the Russian Revolution fascinated him; one had to go with the Stream of History, he said, and that stream was flowing fast toward the dictatorship of the proletariat. He never associated with proletarians, of course, but in a vague and crusty way kept company with the leftward-verging "liberals" of the campus, whose character recently was incisively described by Mr. Colin Clark:

> A desire to have something to worship seems to be the main motive for many liberals, who have specifically denied any other faith. The highly ambiguous meanings of the word "Liberalism" not only provide a broad umbrella under which a diversified and intellectually undisciplined group can comfortably worship together. This is an unintelligent but comparatively harmless piece of opportunism. But in addition the word conveys an esoteric meaning which is rather sinister. Some of those Americans who call themselves Liberals have attributes which make them deservedly unpopular with their fellow-citizens, as anti-religious secularists, or as pro-Soviet fellow-travellers. Reading their literature and listening to their conversations, one must conclude that the word "Liberal" can be used to convey these hidden and unpopular meanings when one is speaking to an initiate, while at the same time the word can be given a much milder meaning if some non-initiate hears and questions it. The obscurity of definition of "Liberalism" in fact appears to be deliberate.[2]

With "liberals" of this stamp, then, Professor Crawley spent some of his time; but it was constitutionally impossible for him to be really part of any clique. The vanity of human wishes was too much with him. He taught his graduate students laboriously; and what he taught them was medieval literature, not the Marxist interpretation of the Middle Ages; for Defecated Research was his god, not the class struggle. It could hardly have occurred to his mind that he had here an opportunity for indoctrination: he was after the Truth himself, in his specialized field, and the means for seeking the Truth was what he taught. Other persons in the faculty of this overgrown college, however, had perceived a mighty effulgence radiating from Moscow; and some of them took advantage of their opportunities, so far as they dared, to indoctrinate their students. It was as much their nature to indoctrinate as it was Professor Crawley's nature to keep his research and his political preferences in separate compartments.

A Marxist Study Club was formed, with faculty sponsors; and the usual quota of fellow-travellers flourished, with, perhaps, here and there an avowed Communist upon the staff; and some students who drank in the pure doctrine of the class struggle later sought positions on the assembly-lines of automobile factories, where they might proselyte fruitfully. One student actually became the prime mover in the Communist conspiracy in British Guiana, some years later. With all this, Dr. Crawley had nothing to do: I believe that he taught the doctrines of no reformer more recent than Piers Plowman.

Then, years after he had ceased to attend Party meetings, he opened his morning paper at breakfast to find himself named, in the headline, as one known to have been a member of a Communist cell at an influential university. Was everything up with him? He hastened to the head of his department, an amiable liberal who wrote reviews for *Science and Society,* and that espouser of liberal causes at once summoned to his aid a professional newspaperman. The grand necessity was to turn away the wrath of legislators and the public before the storm descended. The journalist drew up a Confession of Faith for Professor Crawley; and to it Dr. Crawley put his signature. It was a remarkable document, especially for a professor of literature to have subscribed. In it, Dr. Crawley declared that he had severed any formal ties with the Party years before, which was true; that a little later he had abandoned Marxism thoroughly, which was not; that for some time he had been collaborating with the Federal Bureau of Investigation—which was true (and most alarming news for some colleagues of his), although that collaboration was not voluntary on Professor Crawley's part, perhaps; and that now, with pure patriotism, he taught The American Way of Life in his classes. In this instance, as in many others concerned with suspect professors, what anyone who knew the facts felt, on reading such a declaration, was acute embarrassment mingled with pity. It is so easy to talk of manning the barricades; it is so hard to raise one's voice, really and truly, against a newspaper headline.

Now of course Professor Crawley never taught The American Way of Life in his classes. He did not know what The American Way of Life is, and neither do I. And even if he had believed in some dim ideology of Americanism, he would have been false to his trust as a servant of truth if he had endeavored to indoctrinate students of medieval literature—of all subjects! —in this dim ideology. He would have been as false to his trust as if he had taught The Marxist Way of Life. Professor Crawley, as a genuine scholar, always rose superior to indoctrination; in that he was worthy of academic freedom. But he ceased to be worthy of academic freedom, at least for the moment, when he agreed to pretend that he had been a propagandist for One Hundred Per Cent Americanism. Had he taught Piers Plowman as the forerunner of Thomas Jefferson, and the Rolls Series as the model for the Congressional Record?

After Dr. Crawley's Confession of Faith, written by the newspaperman, was made public, of course Dr. Crawley was quite safe. In private, he told his colleagues how manfully he would behave if ever the House Committee on Un-American Activities, or any other legislative group, should call him to the stand: how he would defy them and shout them down, how he would stand on his rights under the Fifth Amendment, how he would teach tin-horn politicians to interfere with a Pure Scholar. Fortunately for Professor Crawley's heroics, no one ever called him to the stand. By a happy coincidence, the most zealous legislative investigator in those parts happened to have for his constituency the district in which Professor Crawley's college was situated; the college had been kind to the legislator on occasion, prudently offering him the use of certain facilities at the college's disposal; and so the representative of the people observed simply that he was happy that Dr. Crawley taught The American Way of Life, and passed on to other game.

I have discussed this rather saddening affair at some length because I think it illustrates the complexity of our present debate over "subversives in education" and academic freedom. Professor Crawley never was effectively subversive, though he may have wanted to be; he ceased even to try, after a little time; and, whatever sort of Marxist he may or may not have been, as a scholar and a teacher he served the Truth, according to the light that was given. Although I am sorry that Professor Crawley was false to truth in his means of escaping from peril, I am glad that he got off scot-free. He ought not to have been forced out of the Academy. I am describing the scatter-shot method of detecting subversion which plagues us just now. Persons far more deeply implicated than Dr. Crawley have gone quite as scot-free as he did; while persons who probably were no more harmful than he have been discharged, in all probability. The frantic cry that "a reign of terror" paralyzes our educational institutions has been sufficiently refuted by Professor Hook and others. Yet it remains true that our present means of freeing our colleges and universities from totalitarian indoctrinators is ineffectual and sometimes unjust.

At this point, I shall endeavor to lay down some general principles concerning the role of the professor in political controversy and the forming of opinion. The subject has been so warmly discussed in the learned journals and the popular press that I scarcely can hope to make any very original contribution here; all I shall try to do is to criticize and clarify a little.

The general prescriptive right to which scholars and teachers are entitled, in the tradition of academic freedom, is that their political opinions shall be their own concern, and not the concern of the president, or the trustees, or the alumni, or the general public. I do not mean that there are no exceptions possible to this general rule; I mean only that it is the premise upon which we ought to commence our discussion. Academic freedom is a group of immunities and privileges intended to protect the teacher and the scholar from the consequences which often attend marked freedom of thought and expression in the rough world outside the Academy. The teacher and the scholar have laid claim to these immunities and privileges, and the public has allowed the validity of their claim, because here and there, in the hurly-burly of this world of woe, we need to have sanctuaries in which contemplation and speculation may find security; for without such sanctuaries, the life of mind and spirit would flicker out, and the civil social order would slip back toward the primitive night. The teacher and scholar, in the law of medieval England, enjoyed rights called benefit of clergy—that is, a partial exemption from the jurisdiction of secular courts, they being under the jurisdiction of the church, as clerks, or men in orders dedicated to the principle that the fear of God is the beginning of wisdom. I believe that this was a just and wise prerogative, in those times. Then, as now, a good many persons abused the prerogatives of their order; and when criminous clerks behaved intolerably, from time to time, extraordinary measures were employed to recall them to a sense of the duties which were joined to their prerogative. But the general principle endured a great while—indeed, so long as the educated man retained even the most remote association with the religious establishment of England.[3]

Now no one proposes to restore benefit of clergy among us; but I think that academic freedom ought to be a kind of benefit of *clerisy*. The clerisy—a word employed by Coleridge—are all those persons, in any nation, whose duty it is to instruct the people; they are the guardians of knowledge, in all its forms. To be a true guardian of knowledge requires considerable sacrifices, and certain occupational hazards. Academic freedom, or benefit of clerisy, is intended to establish defenses for the body of teachers against the crowd; it is intended to reduce the occupational hazards that dog the duty of speaking the truth. Benefit of clergy often was abused, but it was not abolished until it had lost all meaning. I know that academic freedom is abused, but it ought not to be abolished until it has lost all meaning. It has not lost all meaning among us today; indeed, its meaning and its value are clearer than ever; but it gradually will lose meaning unless the clerisy, the body of teachers and scholars, recognize the duties that accompany their prerogatives, and convince the people that they are fulfilling those duties.

One of the abuses of academic freedom is to convert the liberty of thinking and talking about politics into license. The teacher and scholar ought to be free to speculate about politics, and to make his speculations known, so long as he does not abuse his opportunities by indoctrinating his students, and so long as he does not endeavor to subvert the foundations of society under the cloak of instructing society. It is a principle of English and American jurisprudence and statecraft that we are not compelled to extend freedom to those who would subvert freedom. We may tolerate such persons, true, if we think that, despite their malice, they do not have it in their power to do us much harm. Thus Professor Hook, quite properly, puts less emphasis on the need for expelling Fascists from the col-

leges and universities than upon the necessity for expelling
Communists: the Fascists, at present, are not in a position to
do us much harm. (With bigotry, I think, Dr. Hook puts the
Catholics into the same camp as the Fascists—that is, he tolerates them at present because they seem in no position to enforce their opinions upon the nation. He is laboring under an
historical confusion, I think, assuming as he does that the
Catholic Church of the twentieth century would, if it could,
put into practice the policies of the Catholic establishment
in the days of Reformation and Counter-Reformation.) But
neither natural right nor logic compels us invariably to tolerate, in all circumstances, the people who would not tolerate us
in their hour of triumph. If, then, we tolerate the abuse of
academic freedom by those who substitute indoctrination for
true teaching and design to overthrow the very order which
gives them their being, we do so only because we feel secure
from the malice of these people, and think it better to endure
their abuses than to tamper with the general operation of the
rules of academic freedom. There are times, however, when
we are compelled to suspend this toleration in order to secure
our liberties. It is not necessarily true that Truth always will
prevail in "a free market of ideas"; if, indolently, we permit the
enemies of Truth to secure the gates and the stalls of that
market-place, they may drive us out of it altogether, as they
did in Germany for a time and as they have done in Russia.

There are limits to just toleration. Members of the clerisy
may commit abuses for which they deserve to be expelled
from the order of the clerisy. Our problem, in this, is to reconcile a general solicitude for tolerance with a decent vigilance
in behalf of enduring freedom of thought and expression. We
need to avoid what Paul Elmer More called "the demon of
the absolute". Scholars and teachers do not have an absolute
right to do and say whatever they please, in disregard of the
duties of their order, any more than criminous clerks had a
right to lay about them as they pleased in defiance of all law.

We ought to guarantee them as much freedom as we possibly can, and to tolerate abuses of that freedom so far as we safely can. But they do not enjoy an absolute liberty to subvert liberty. They do not have the right to deny all rights. They are not entrusted with the privilege of teaching society so that they may teach society to corrupt itself. I have said earlier that I think Professor Hook goes too far in the definition of academic freedom which he offers. (In practice, Mr. Hook establishes very definite restrictions of that definition, and he reasons prudently therein.) Professionally qualified persons, Mr. Hook says, are privileged by academic freedom "to inquire, discover, publish and teach the truth as they see it in their field of competence, without any control or authority except the control or authority of the rational methods by which truth is established." He thinks that academic freedom acknowledges discipline or restraint only when such controls are exerted by "the community of qualified scholars". Now I believe that certain other authorities have a right to exercise some control over academic freedom. I believe that academic freedom owes a decent respect to the consensus of opinion of the ages and the prevailing opinions of the age in which the community of qualified scholars exists. I believe that academic freedom owes a loyalty to the moral order which transcends the foibles of human reason. I believe that academic freedom may properly be restrained, in some degree, by the right of any society to ensure its own preservation. I do not think that the community of scholars (which, at any one time, may be mistaken as a body, or rather which may be misled by the temporarily dominant majority in that community) is always a law unto itself. I doubt, for instance, that the community of scholars has an unqualified right to tamper with every prescriptive moral value, as Professor H. S. Commager implies when, in *Freedom, Loyalty, Dissent*, he writes that "we must encourage experimentation even in the moral realm."[4] On the contrary, I share Burke's opinion that "the great mysterious incorporation

116

of the human race", taken as the expression of the experience of men over many centuries, has a right to assert itself, in time of peril, against the sophist and the calculator:

> We know that *we* have made no discoveries; and we think that no discoveries are to be made, in morality; nor many in the great principles of government, nor in the ideas of liberty, which were understood long before we were born, altogether as well as they will be after the grave has heaped its mould upon our presumption, and the silent tomb shall have imposed its law on our pert loquacity.

In short, I am of the opinion that in politics, as in other fields of knowledge, limitations may be imposed upon academic freedom for the sake of preserving academic freedom. I think that legislative bodies have a right to try to prevent members of the community of scholars who abuse their privileges from corrupting the whole body of scholars and the nation at large. But I hope that we will exercise that power of control over the excesses of academic freedom with the greatest circumspection and prudence. To return to my example, the case of Professor Crawley, my opinion is that we ought to tolerate people like Professor Crawley, and even to cherish them; but we ought not to tolerate scholars and teachers who, passing beyond the eccentricities of Dr. Crawley, turn their liberty into license, and so endanger our liberty. It is a question of degree and expediency. And we have the right to expect of Dr. Crawley and men like him that if they are to enjoy the privileges of the clerisy, they must act consistently as members of the clerisy, speaking the truth even when their worldly prosperity is at stake, and not conforming servilely to the passions of the hour. Scholars and teachers are not invested with their immunities that they may echo the slogans of the mob. No one can guarantee them *absolute* security; academic freedom, like all other freedoms, never is utterly secure; and if the scholars do not stand up for their own integrity, no one else is going to persevere in the endeavor to protect men who will not protect themselves.

In the section of this chapter which follows, then, I shall quarrel with two bodies of opinion on the political rights and duties of the clerisy. One camp is that of the indoctrinators, and that camp is made up of men with radically opposed notions of what doctrines ought to be made orthodox: the band of things-as-they-are, represented by Mr. William Buckley, Jr.; and the band of the social reconstructionists, dominated by one faction of the disciples of John Dewey. (In this latter group I do not mean to include Professor Hook and his friends.) The other camp is that of the doctrinaire liberals, among whom are Professor Commager, Mr. Hutchins, and certain spokesmen for the Association of University Professors. I think that the partisans of the first camp would undo academic freedom, in its political aspect, by excessive regulation; I think that the partisans of the second camp would leave academic freedom naked unto its enemies, in its political aspect, by tolerating license.

2

In the eyes of the Indoctrinators, the scholar and teacher are servants, hired for money to do a job. In the eyes of the Doctrinaire Liberals, the scholar and the teacher are masterless men, rather like Cain, and ought to remain so. In my eyes, the scholar and the teacher are Bearers of the Word—that is, the conservators and promulgators of knowledge in all its forms; they are neither simply hired functionaries nor simply knights-errant in the lists.

First I shall say something about the position of the Indoctrinators of Things-as-They-Are, whose most able representative seems to be Mr. William F. Buckley, Jr. Mr. Buckley, near the end of his forthright book, informs us that one thing is

118

clear: "It is time that honest and discerning scholars cease to manipulate the term academic freedom for their own ends and in such fashion as to deny the rights of individuals. For in the last analysis, academic freedom must mean the freedom of men and women to supervise the educational activities and aims of the schools they oversee and support."[5] Really, we ought not to be in love with paradoxes. One might as well say that the freedom against self-incrimination, at trials, means the freedom of the judge to interrogate whoever he likes however he likes, and so keep himself free from any share in the guilt. Academic freedom did not arise as a protection to the constituted authorities who have in their charge the property of a university. Such trustees run few risks. Academic freedom in the world of learning, like profit in the world of business, is the reward of risk. The risk which the scholar and the teacher run is the risk of being reprimanded or discharged by persons intolerant of frank expression. To compensate the entrepreneur for the risk of financial loss, profit exists; to compensate the clerisy for the risk of security, academic freedom exists. Academic freedom, like profit, sometimes proves to be more of an aspiration than a reality. But as few entrepreneurs would risk their resources in business without some hope of true profit, so few scholars and teachers would risk their reputations and their livelihood without some hope of freedom to think and to speak. In the interest of the conservation and the promulgation of truth, then, the "men and women who oversee and support" the Academy are wise if they cherish academic freedom and interfere as little as possible with what is thought and said in the institutions of which they are guardians—although they are not the only guardians. I hope that among such trustees are persons of learning and penetration; on the board of Yale Corporation, I am sure, such persons always are to be found, although I am afraid that the same cannot be said with any confidence of many of the elected boards and trustees of state institutions. But it is improbable that any one of these trustees knows more than the whole body of professors of the university; and few of these trustees have so much time for reflection, or so direct acquaintance with the art of teaching, as the better professors. When Mr. Buckley, then, demands that boards of trustees, and alumni associations, exact a conformity to certain doctrines from all scholars and teachers, I am afraid that he must take the position that persons outside the Academy know more about what the Academy ought to do than persons inside the Academy; and I think this position is untenable.

I do not think that the scholar and the teacher ought to be looked upon by the trustees of educational institutions as mere servants, hired for a wage to preach fixed doctrines. We have had altogether too much expression of that point of view in the United States of America. I think that the trustees, instead, ought to look upon the scholar and the teachers as persons who have honored the university by consenting to give that institution the benefit of their wisdom, ordinarily serving for a salary that is really simply an honorarium. We tend to become what people think we are; and if the scholar and the professor are treated as persons of dignity and integrity, dedicated to the Truth, in time almost all of them will conduct themselves as persons of dignity and integrity, dedicated to the Truth. If, on the other hand, they are treated as servants, they will come to display the vices attributed to servants; and since they never will be well-paid servants, we shall not be able to expect from them as much dignity or integrity as we obtain from plumber-servants or barber-servants, who are better paid in proportion to the nature of the work required of them.

Now the doctrines which Mr. Buckley wants promulgated in the Academy are two: faith in Christianity, and individualism. I personally agree that the first of these is a good thing, and I think that Mr. Buckley knows what he means by it. I do *not* agree that "individualism" is a good thing, and I do not think that Mr. Buckley knows what he means by it. In truth, any professor who attempted to indoctrinate his students in *both* Christianity and individualism would be hopelessly inconsistent; for individualism is anti-Christian. It is possible logically to be a Christian, and possible logically to be an individualist; it is not possible to be the two simultaneously. My first objection to Mr. Buckley's scheme, then, is that he himself really does not know what he wants these professor-servants to teach.

My second objection is that, even were it generally agreed that these two objectives were wise, such an attempt to make up men's minds about them by indoctrination would be the worst possible way to accomplish the desired end. Faith, like love, cannot be forced. Once it should become reasonably clear that the professor-servants, one and all, were deliberately bent upon indoctrination, then the students, and everyone else of liberal mind, would be so vexed that probably they would go over to the opposite extreme, by a natural reaction. The only way in which the student-body and the public could be compelled to accept this pabulum is the way adopted by the Nazi and Communist regimes: to forbid any other teaching and to utilize all the powers of the state to efface even the memory of any alternative modes of thought. Such a policy would be quite as repugnant to Mr. Buckley as to me.

Though this chapter is concerned principally with political opinion, I shall digress for a moment, to touch upon religious opinion. I think that Mr. Hook is wrong in holding that the study of religion has no place in the university; I think that Mr. Buckley is wrong in holding that religious faith ought to be exacted of professors and students. Agreeing with Newman that theology is the queen of the sciences and that religion is the most important of all subjects in the university, I think that the cause of religion would be done an incalculable disservice if any attempt were made to cram it down people's throats. Such is not often the method of the better Catholic or Episcopalian or Presbyterian or Methodist or Quaker institutions of learning. Some of these, I know, have drifted so far away from any doctrinal system that religion, with them, remains only a sort of sentimental aura suffusing the curriculum; but even this error is better than the opposite error of "dinging the pulpit to blads", as John Knox (though not in a university) used to do. Professor Hoxie Neal Fairchild puts this matter very well:

> It would be absurd to advocate the indoctrination of all students with a single official philosophy. The necessary consensus does not exist, and even if it did exist it should not be imposed arbitrarily. The college should be a community of inquirers—some called students, some called teachers—each of whom is striving to arrive at a philosophy. What the individual discovers may be very new or very old; it may be congenial or repugnant to the majority of his fellows. The far-away goal is unity, but it must be sought in and through the diversity which now actually exists. The quest entails historical investigation and critical evaluation, in an atmosphere of complete freedom, candor, and disinterestedness, of all the great normative hypotheses now available for thinking men.
>
> No one will deny that religion has been the supreme integrator of intellectual and emotional experience, or that the subsidence of religious faith and the consequent chasm between intellectual and spiritual life are largely responsible for the predicament of modern man. Those who hold that it has become desirable or necessary to do without religion must at least be prepared to describe what it is they are abandoning and what they propose to substitute for it. At present there is a marked revival of religion among members of the intellectual class. Whether this is a retreat from reason or a reassertion of the possibility of reason is a debatable question. By all means, then, let it be debated.[6]

I have no relish for Justice Holmes' phrase "free trade in ideas" to describe the high dignity of independent thought which ought to prevail in the Academy. Scholars and teachers are not traffickers in a market, but members of the clerisy; and the greatest of their concerns is what Burke calls "the contract of eternal society"—which, Burke goes on to say, is not to be considered as "nothing better than a partnership agreement in a trade of pepper and coffee, calico or tobacco, or some other such low concern, to be taken up for a little temporary interest, and to be dissolved by the fancy of the parties." But the Academy will not succeed in conserving or in advancing the Truth unless it encourages and protects full and free discussion even of the most important topics. And I do not think that the cause of religious belief need fear the effects of debate, in these times. I repeat that the functions of the Academy are two: the conservation of truth, and the extension of it. If ever a choice has to be made, the Academy ought to choose to conserve the known truth, rather than to discard what we already have on the chance that we might conceivably get something better out of rootless speculation. This choice does *not* have to be made today in the matter of religious knowledge, however; what the cause of religious knowledge chiefly needs is a fair hearing; nothing could do that cause greater mischief than to attempt to advance it by indoctrination, especially in the Academy.

Some of these objections apply also to Mr. Buckley's second doctrine, individualism. If one really wants individualism, the reprehension of individuality in the Academy is scarcely the means for attaining conformity to that system of thought. How, for that matter, we are to promote the cause of individualism by exacting conformity to unalterable "individualistic" principles, I am unable to fathom. But I do not think that Mr. Buckley really knows the meaning of the political term *individualism*; if he did, he would not want it. Individualism, the ideology called individualism, "was born in hell; and look to it, for some of you shall be the father." It is a denial that life has any meaning except gratification of the ego; in politics, it must end in anarchy; its philosophers are Godwin, Hodgskin, and Spencer. It is not possible for one man to be both Christian and Individualist. I am aware that the word has been loosely used, even by scholars like Professor F. A. Hayek; but it has a clear historical definition. Now I do not think that Mr. Buckley really wants us to be indoctrinated in this ideology. What he is talking about, when he writes "Individualism", is a complex of social principles: conservative statecraft, private property, free enterprise, constitutional government, representative institutions, and the like. But rhetoric may corrupt men, as Mr. Richard Weaver tells us; and if we believe in these principles, we ought not to lump them together as "individualism" and make that into a god-term. Mr. Buckley wants to be conservative; and conservatism is the negation of ideology; so I think it is dangerous for him to hanker after an abstract Individualism to be preached at students.

I have said that Christianity and Individualism are inconsonant. I do not mean that Christianity and conservative statecraft, or private property, or free enterprise, or constitutional government, or representative institutions, are inconsonant. On the contrary, I think that Mr. Buckley is protesting against a misinterpretation of the "social gospel" when he objects to religious teaching that is no more than sentimental humanitarianism, an amorphous pity, which thinks that the terrestrial paradise can be created by the state. Such a "Christian social gospel" is opposed to true Christian charity. "Statists that labour to contrive a commonwealth without poverty," Sir Thomas Browne observes, "take away the object of our charity; not understanding only the commonwealth of a Christian, but forgetting the prophecy of Christ." Mr. Buckley does right to protest against this decline of religious faith into a mere moralized collectivism.

If I have been hard on Mr. Buckley here, it is because I think his book worth reading, and because (with Professor Hook) I think that most of Mr. Buckley's adversaries have assailed him for the wrong reasons. Many of his critics implied that he must be some sort of totalitarian. Nothing could be further from the truth: Mr. Buckley is sincerely attached to something far removed from the totalitarian state, and something much better than Individualism. What he really desires is the preservation of American religious faith, constitutional government, and free economic institutions. But his program of indoctrination, accomplished by a rigid enforcement of secular dogmas upon professor-servants, would be ruinous to his aims. Mr. Buckley is much opposed to "Keynesianism". I do not know just what Keynesianism amounts to, though I have read the principal works of John Maynard Keynes. No man was less of an ideologue than Lord Keynes. This economist was fertile in ideas, not all of them internally consistent. As for his plan to moderate fluctuations of the business-cycle by inflationary and deflationary policies of government, he seems to have reckoned without the pressure that the masses, in the modern democratic state, constantly exert upon government always to pursue inflation and never deflation. But all this certainly is a legitimate realm of speculation. If professors may not talk about the ideas of Keynes, whose ideas may they discuss? What economist ever arrived at complete and unalterable truth about every aspect of economic being? Not Smith, certainly, nor Ricardo, nor Marshall. Both to conserve and to extend knowledge, professors of political economy ought to be expected to discuss the ideas of Keynes and many others. It is true that they ought not to expound Keynes' principles as unalterable secular dogmas, either. I am sure that Mr. Buckley has met with professors who did just that, though I am equally sure that Yale has fewer ideologues of every description than nearly any other university in America. I repeat, however, that we must prepare to endure some abuse of academic freedom in order to gain the benefits of intelligent speculation for which the Academy exists. If we meet with no worse abuses than an excess of enthusiasm for John Maynard Keynes, we are fortunate. If the members of university faculties flirted with varieties of collectivism in recent years, still we need to remind ourselves that the Academy is subject, though it tries to rise above popular passion, to the same general climate of opinion as the general public. If members of university faculties are to be won to the cause of conserving traditional society, they will be persuaded only by other members of the clerisy, not dragooned into preaching what they do not believe to students who will not believe them. I sympathize with all Mr. Buckley's indignation at finding the principles to which he subscribes treated contemptuously by some professors at Yale; but I think he would find his remedy worse than the disease. There is every reason why a vigorous and intelligent university graduate like Mr. Buckley should protest in writing against the domination of university faculties by persons with whose opinions he disagrees; but there is every reason why he should not attempt to remedy this condition by recommending a rigid surveillance of all professors' work in the lecture-room by trustees and alumni. I think that Mr. Buckley suffers from the debating-society habit of having to recommend "practical remedial action". Really, the only way to counter the teaching of fallacies is to do a better job of teaching truths.

Now I do not think that Mr. Buckley really desires to subject us to indoctrination; indeed, more than once he says that all he desires is a fair field for the view he favors. But he slips into the habit of writing as if he would merely supplant what a professor of history at the University of California calls "the liberal terror" by the "individualist" terror. And I am afraid that, in practice, a program of studies subjected to formal review with respect to its conformity to the presumed views of founders and alumni would tend toward servility even more than the half-unconscious type of indoctrination which is conducted by professors who, secure in a dim liberal orthodoxy, speak with contempt of other points of view. Since we cannot know the heart, we must judge men by their words, ordinarily, and some of Mr. Buckley's words are imprudent.

I turn now to the other school of Indoctrinators, whom Mr.

Buckley would detest: the Social Reconstructionists. Mr. Mortimer Smith recently gave some account of them in *The Diminished Mind*. In general, they propose to make education, at every level, into an instrument for ensuring the triumph of equalitarian collectivism, dominated by an administrative elite; they talk a great deal about "democracy", but, as Mr. Hook points out, by this they mean only a social tableland of which these new Jacobins will be the masters; in their scheme is no place for individuality, or volition, or genuine representation of the people. Indoctrination of the sort which Mr. Buckley recommends would be ridiculously liberal by the side of the indoctrination which Professor Theodore Brameld and his associates recommend. The Academy would become simply the upper level of this machine for ensuring conformity to the new order. Scholars and teachers, under this system, would be not merely servants, but slaves. Of course they would be servants of the "state", or the "people", nominally; in actuality, as in Russia, they would be the servants of the governing clique. They, far more than Mr. Buckley, are devotees of what Professor Hook accurately describes as "political religion".

A moderate specimen of this political religion is Mr. J. P. Williams' article "The Schoolmen and Religion", in *School and Society* (August 13, 1949). Mr. Williams, convinced that traditional religious instruction in the schools ought to be forbidden, nevertheless recognizes the need for some spiritual or ethical belief in any society; and he proposes to substitute for "trying to get belief in God indoctrinated at public expense" his own program of a secular faith to touch upon "the spiritual problems of our whole people." In substance, his scheme is simply Positivism brought up to date, and bears many marks of the totalitarian regime which Comte sketched. This social religion will deal with "the basic ethical propositions on which society is founded. Unless these ethical principles attain the level of religious conviction, they lack staying power and society is endangered by every demagogue who manifests the power to awaken religious fervor." Mr. Williams' real concern, it appears, is not really to make men religious, but to make it impossible for them to believe in traditional religion, so that "demagogues" like celebrated preachers may not remind them of an order superior to the equalitarian state. Knowing that humankind will not abide a vacuum, he is eager to fill up the abyss created by the ejection of religious instruction from the schools with his new positivistic creed. He prescribes "Systematic and universal indoctrination", to give permanence to the New Order. This religon shall worship Demos, democracy (at least in name) being the basis of the new society. Like the myths which Plato suggested might be taught by the Guardians in his ideal state, a set of values will be drilled into the young, "believed to be ultimate in its nature and . . . taken on faith." The object will be not truth, but conformity: "The youth of America must be brought to the conviction that democracy is the very Law of Life, and that conduct in accord with that Law of Life will in the end prove more satisfying than conduct which runs counter to democracy." Indeed, Mr. Williams speaks of investing Demos not only with a metaphysical sanction, but a supernatural sanction into the bargain.

Here "democracy", as with John Dewey and Sidney Hook, is considered an end in itself, not a means to an end. There is no word of liberty, or order, or justice, or peace, or even happiness. Freedom of thought and expression is not worth mentioning: the great aim of the Academy will be to tell men lies, if necessary, in order to persuade them to merge their personalities in the drab society which Mr. Williams calls "democracy". Mr. Williams and his friends have arrived at final and complete truth: all that matters is Democracy (so long as Mr. Williams and colleagues guide that democracy), and no dissent will be tolerated. We are back with Lenin: "Liberty? What for? What for?" If the terrestrial paradise has been attained, to think of liberty is treasonable.

Such a "democracy" would be leaderless and mindless. Even the best of democracies, restrained by constitutional guarantees and representative institutions and the influence of traditional religion, needs constantly to stimulate, rather than repress, variety of opinion and freedom of speculation. Otherwise it will soon cease to be a democracy. And any society which thinks it has reached perfection has really reached caducity. A silent tyranny of the majority over active and speculative intellects is a vice toward which all democracies incline, and from which their well-wishers will do everything in their power to redeem them. Tocqueville describes forebodingly this danger:

> In America the majority raises formidable barriers around the liberty of opinion; within these barriers an author may write what he pleases, but woe to him if he goes beyond them. Not that he is in danger of an auto-da-fé, but he is exposed to continued obloquy and persecution. His political career is closed forever, since he has offended the only authority that is able to open it. Every sort of compensation, even that of celebrity, is refused to him. Before making public his opinions he thought he had sympathizers; now it seems to him that he has none any more since he revealed himself to everyone; then those who blame him criticize loudly and those who think as he does keep quiet and move away without courage. He yields at length, overcome by the daily effort which he has to make, and subsides into silence, as if he felt remorse for having spoken the truth.[7]

A democracy of elevation will contend in every way it can against this silent tyranny, which would stifle *individuality* (as contrasted with the cult of Individualism). The scheme of the Social Reconstructionists, fatal to the Academy, in short order would be fatal to democracy as well; for societies are not preserved and renewed by men indoctrinated from their earliest years in a dismal secular orthodoxy of equalitarianism.

Professor Sidney Hook is one of the most able and relentless opponents of indoctrination in "democracy", or in anything else. Such a proposal as the one I have described above, he says, "is in fact the hallmark of illiberalism in education—and this remains true irrespective of whether an educator wants to use public education to teach the necessity of 'a thoroughly reconstituted domestic economy' or the necessity of a thoroughly stabilized *status quo* capitalist economy, whether he takes as his grand design 'international world government' or rampant American chauvinism, whether it is the 'old deal' or the 'new deal.' "[8] Yet even Mr. Hook endorses Dr. Conant's proposal that the theory and practice of official Communism should be made a required study in the curriculum of all colleges; and he would add to this the study of democracy "as a way of life".[9] I do not totally disagree with these proposals, though I trust that Mr. Hook, at least, means that every college should adopt such a program at its own volition, not upon instructions from some political authority. I think it worth remarking, however, that the American Bar Association recently received a resolution recommending the former proposal, and, after debate, rejected it. The Bar Association is not to be suspected of any sympathy with Communism; but the mind of the lawyer usually is on guard against indoctrination. The very titles of these projected courses might tend to lead the teacher and the student toward ideology, rather than rational inquiry. I am very much in favor of sound study of political and social institutions in our colleges; but I am inclined to think that required courses of this sort, isolated from the historical and ethical and religious disciplines, would slide ominously toward the indoctrination which Professor Hook dislikes quite as much as I do.

Though the criticism of the Indoctrinators might profitably be pursued much further, I propose now to examine briefly the camp of the Doctrinaire Liberals; and here, too, I shall take common ground with Professor Hook, on occasion. Ideologists like Mr. Theodore Brameld and Mr. J. P. Williams think of the Academy as an institution where young people are taught to chorus equalitarian slogans like that of the sheep in *Nineteen-Eighty-Four:* "Four legs good, two legs bad." Doctrinaire liberals like Mr. H. S. Commager and Mr. Harold Taylor think of the Academy as a place where professors, like the Sophists, talk perpetually of the impossibility of knowing anything with certitude, and the necessity for considering every point of view, and the need for being ever so liberal. These latter gentlemen put me in mind of Bacon's famous line: "What is truth? said jesting Pilate, and would not stay for an answer."

"Is education in a democracy designed to teach the young to obey authority?" President Taylor of Sarah Lawrence College inquires. He thinks not. "That is what deprived the German youth of its independence and gave them Nazism. American education is designed to teach the young to be free, to teach them to accept no authority except one founded on reason, respect for the human mind, tolerance, law, justice, and the ideals of freedom."[10] Now it is a most reckless assertion, unworthy of a college president, that German youth were "given Nazism" because German education inculcated some respect for authority. One might as well say that Germany was given Nazism because the Weimar Republic had a federal constitution, or because women were allowed to vote; the *non sequitur* is no more startling.* The most obvious reason why German youth were given Nazism is that German liberals and conservatives and socialists tolerated the Nazi movement until it was too late to prevent a *coup d'etat.* It was the old-school German, who believed in just authority, that found the courage to try to overthrow the Nazis, and so destroyed himself. Reasoning of this character may well make us doubt President Taylor's declaration that we need have no fear of the Communists in our country, and may safely go about our educational task of doubting all things and denying all prescriptive values and teaching American youth that ambivalence is the

---

* For a valuable criticism of German and American education, see Professor W. E. Hocking's *Experiment in Education.*

mark of an educated man. Are we to be allowed no respect for the wisdom of our ancestors, or the lessons of history, or traditional morality, or our own duly constituted representatives in this Republic? Apparently not: Dr. Taylor has nothing but contempt for the endeavors of Congress and the state legislatures to inquire into Communist conspiracy. But I seem to remember that a principal aid to the Nazis in their rise to power was their utilization and encouragement of contempt for parliamentary institutions and democratic representatives. Professor T. V. Smith, a scholar well known for the liberality of his opinions, disposes rather thoroughly of gentlemen like Mr. Taylor, who would have us rely solely upon private judgment and an invincible confidence that all will go well if only we encourage every man to follow his own humor:

"But give the politicians an inch, and they'll take a mile!" Only upon the assumption that they are our enemies. I assume that they are our friends, and I am recommending that basic assumption as touching not only the politicians but all the indispensable functionaries in our capitalistic democracy. As teachers, the worst of all things that can befall us, whether in the name of academic freedom or otherwise, is for us to extrapolate our fears into making us regard as enemies those with whom we must, willy-nilly, cooperate. In our zeal to make academic freedom cover party-member Communists at the present juncture, we alienate those with whom we must work, in the fatuous behalf of those who will never work with us. It is surely a shortsighted liberalism which gets us thus offsided to our friends. Politicians who put themselves beyond the pale are not mentioned, nor should be called by name; for free publicity is what they live upon.

My general conclusion is that what we academicians have mostly to fear today is our fears; but that is enough to do us great professional disservice. Admitting the need of watchfulness along a wide front, I reaffirm . . . that academic freedom commits us to circumspection but does not reward or require suspicion. Our economic system is a capitalistic economy, and we must put ourselves inside our system, not outside it, if we are to convert our professional freedom from something negative into something positive. Our political system is a representative government, and we must put ourselves inside that ambit, not outside it, if we are to convert our freedom into something affirmative. Our religious system is Judeo-Christian, and we must put ourselves inside that Weltanschauung, not outside it, if we are to further our common spiritual ends.[11]

Mr. Taylor has a distinguished defender, however: Professor H. S. Commager, who reviewed President Taylor's book *On Education and Freedom* in the *New York Times Book Review* (April 4, 1954). Dr. Commager regretted that Mr. Taylor had had to take so much time writing about communism in the colleges: "For communism in the colleges is a little like the Emperor's new clothes. So far, as Mr. Taylor points out, almost a decade of incessant snooping has discovered two real live Communists in American colleges or universities, and no evidence was submitted that either of these ever misused his position to infect or subvert students."

Professor Commager's remarks in praise of President Taylor recall a quip concerning two distinguished English scholars:

> *Ladling butter from alternate tubs,*
> *Stubbs butters Freeman, Freeman butters Stubbs.*

For Mr. Commager, in *Freedom, Loyalty, Dissent,* is quite as sure as Mr. Taylor that a genuine Communist is as rare in American colleges as a genuine witch. The state or city that conducts a campaign against Communists, Professor Commager actually writes, "very rarely finds any, and it rarely finds any subversives unless it wants to stretch that term to embrace anyone who rejoiced in Russian victories in 1943 or who reads *The Nation* or who favors socialized medicine."[12]

Professor Hook, in his review of Mr. Commager's book in the *New Republic,* so pitilessly drove Mr. Commager from pillar to post on this score that I hesitate, out of very pity, to undertake any further demolition of Mr. Commager's poor little

battered and broken book. Yet I cannot avoid remarking that
in the New York City school system alone, since 1951, thirty
teachers have been dismissed because of their Communist affiliations, eighteen have been dismissed because of their refusal to testify before Congressional committees, and fifty-two
more have admitted past membership in the Communist
party. At present, 120 teachers there are to be questioned.
This takes no account of fellow-travellers. The number of persons whose positions have been lost or are in jeopardy seems
to vary according to what doctrinaire liberal one happens to
read. Mr. Robert Hutchins, writing for *Look*, laments that
"Senator William E. Jenner says that twenty or more colleges
and universities in California are co-operating with state and
Congressional investigating groups in a blacklisting program
under which about 100 members of their faculties have been
removed and at least as many more rejected for teaching
posts."[13] In this, as in so much else, the doctrinaire liberals
are ambivalent. If only a few Communists are discovered,
then an investigation was pointless cruelty; if many are turned
out, then the nation is said to have been exposed to the full
fury of a ruthless witch-hunt. Mr. Hutchins, indeed, is so concerned that "Hardly a day passes that I do not feel pusillani-
mous, because I must now refuse to associate myself with
anything, even the movement for Mother's Day, without
knowing the political views of every other person who is associated or who may later become associated with the movement."[14] How are the mighty fallen! Only Bertrand Russell
exceeds Mr. Hutchins in his alarm for American liberties:
Lord Russell says that it is dangerous to quote Thomas Jefferson in the United States. But we are descending into bathos.

This terror of national and state legislators is interestingly
offset, among the doctrinaire liberals, by a tranquil confidence
that subversive persons are rare as robins in December. Consider this astounding piece of naïveté or disingenousness on
Professor Commager's part—he is writing early in 1954, long

after the exposure of the Institute of Pacific Relations: he re-
monstrates against "Senator McCarthy's assault upon the
State Department and particularly upon Professor Lattimore
and other Far Eastern experts", and repeats the words of Senator Tydings that Mr. McCarthy's charges against Mr. Lattimore were "a fraud and a hoax perpetrated on the Senate of
the United States and the American people." Well! Do none
of us read the newspapers, or the reports of Congressional
committees? The fact that Mr. Lattimore has not yet been
convicted of perjury does not convert him into Nathan Hale.
A man who can still believe in the integrity of Owen Lattimore would maintain the chastity of Messalina. Mr. Lattimore
indeed was not "the top Soviet espionage agent in the United
States"; as Mr. Irving Kristol observes, he was much more
valuable to the Soviets as their unofficial ambassador.[15] Mr.
Lattimore's role is sufficiently traced in Mr. James Burnham's
The Web of Subversion; and the indifference to truth displayed by the Tydings Committee is detailed in Mr. Buckley's
and Mr. Bozell's *McCarthy and his Enemies,* a fact acknowledged by the most hostile critics of that book. Bearing in mind
Professor Commager's distress over the inaccuracies committed by Congressmen, how are we to regard his remarkable
charity toward Mr. Lattimore? One is puzzled to understand
just what sort of person Mr. Commager would confess to be
subversive. Is it necessary to manufacture hand-grenades in
one's attic to come under the surveillance of Congress?

Now I think that what the doctrinaire liberals—more properly called disintegrated liberals, perhaps—like Mr. Commager and Mr. Taylor and Mr. Hutchins fear is really, in their
heart of hearts, themselves. Their neat little world of Progress and Civil Liberties Committees and Welfare Legislation
and Goodness of Humankind has dissolved, overnight, into
its constituent atoms. They are lost in a dark wood, and they
cry out in terror at every shadow. They are the Displaced
Persons of the realm of the American intellect. Uncertain now

of their own first principles, they nevertheless utter shrilly their old slogans, as if by force of repetition they could give them fresh life. They are democrats, and they denounce the constituted representatives of the people; they are liberals, and they mourn for the liberties of totalitarians. Confronted by the Soviet ogre, they insist that they are in imminent danger of being swallowed up by Republican Congressmen. Mr. William J. Newman describes their plight accurately; American liberalism of the sort they espoused is bemused:

> Increasingly driven back upon its contradiction between individualism and *étatisme,* its slogans either irrelevant or dully repetitive, and its opponents greedily picking its bones, it has lost its hold as a picture of life as it is and should be. . . . Those who cling to it do as the shipwrecked man does to a raft—desperately, but without much idea of where it will take him. Others have abandoned it with much rhetorical flourish. Still others have lost their clear vision and find it reduced to a golden mist of abstractions.[16]

The reader may have gathered that I do not much respect the present opinions of the doctrinaire liberals on the subject of academic freedom. I do not think that their views are so baneful as those of the Indoctrinators, but I fear that if we took their moans of anguish very seriously, we would run the risk of losing the reality of academic freedom by slipping into license. We ought, indeed, to make sure that in expelling from the ranks of the clerisy such persons as have lost their right to the benefits of academic freedom, we do not impair the principle itself. The doctrinaire liberal, however, recognizes almost no standard to which the clerisy ought to conform. The theme of Professor Commager's little book is that everyone ought always to dissent from everything for dissension's sake. This, he informs us, will produce strength of character and freedom of mind: "As William Ellery Channing said over a century ago, 'We have conservatives

enough.' "[17] What Mr. Commager ignores in this pronounce-
ment is that it was uttered over a century ago. Mr. Commager
is living in the last century. Since then, conservatives have
been extirpated in a very great part of the world; certain
things need to be conserved now, not taken to pieces like old
toys; and one of those things is academic freedom. The pity
of it is that we have so few true conservators of liberty and
justice left.

Professor Commager's philosophical confusion, sufficiently
representative of the "liberalism" that refuses to take a stand
against anything radical or in favor of anything conservative—
the liberalism typified by the fatuous motto of the French
parliamentary factions devoted to neoterism, "No enemies to
the Left"—is best described in his own words:

> The most distinctively American philosophies have been tran-
> scendentalism—which is the philosophy of the Higher Law—
> and pragmatism—which is the philosophy of experimentation
> and pluralism. These two principles are the very core of Ameri-
> canism: the principle of the Higher Law, or of obedience to the
> dictates of conscience rather than of statutes, and the principle of
> pragmatism, or the rejection of a single good and of the notion
> of a finished universe. From the beginning Americans have
> known that there were new worlds to conquer, new truths to be
> discovered. Every effort to confine Americanism to a single pat-
> tern, to constrain it to a single formula, is disloyalty to every-
> thing that is valid in Americanism.[18]

One principal trouble with this theory is that the two philosophies Mr. Commager adores both are extremes, and are
at opposite poles. If Mr. Commager believes in both, he will
always be hopelessly ambivalent. Neither one is a safe shelter
for academic freedom. America, truly, has flourished through
diversity, not through uniformity; what Mr. Commager rel-
ishes, however, is a "liberal" uniformity. To advocate dissent
for its own sake, to cry up the pleasures of perpetual doubt,
may be well enough in a time when a genial orthodoxy pre-

serves the dissenter on principle from the retaliation of those
great grim powers that keep watch upon human presumption.
But dissent is possible only when the framework of assent is
sound. In times when the fountains of the great deep are
broken up, to revile the remnants of prescription at the very
moment a merciless domination threatens conservative and
liberal alike is an act of childish impudence. It is an act not of
academic freedom, but of academic license. We can afford
to tolerate such acts only if a good many of us still hold by
some strong affirmation. The Communist, we are told, pitiable
hunted wretch, is a harmless creature, and perhaps a very
good fellow, dedicated to experimentation; the constituted
representative of the American people is a glowering bully.
What folly! Mr. Commager's Loyal American is a perpetual
non-conformist, regardless of circumstances; he loves nothing
but change, and acknowledges no master but his appetite for
asserting his liberal individuality. We cannot too often repair
to Mill's *Liberty*, Mr. Commager reminds us—Mill's *Liberty*,
written with a guileless faith in sweet reasonableness and the
inevitability of progress. How very old-fashioned a man Mr.
Commager is, positively charming in his antique simplicities.
Mill thought that the only considerable peril the future held
was that of a dull conformity to public opinion, in the utilitarian tranquillity of the dawning age, which was to be one
vast Victorian England spread over all the universe; therefore
the chief service a rational man could perform would be to
behave eccentrically on principle. The most recent critic of
Mill's mind, Mr. R. P. Anschutz, disposes of Mr. Commager,
rather in Professor T. V. Smith's vein:

> But this is simply to substitute one error for another—bohemian
> nonsense for bourgeois nonsense. Whatever the capacities of
> any man, in any walk of life, he will necessarily spend a large
> part of his time in assimilating the traditions of his calling. After
> that he is usually engaged in a perpetual struggle to be equal
> to them. It is this which provides the content of his individuality.

The assumption of the sort of self-sufficiency that Mill recommends will prevent him from attaining any individuality at all. Nor is the case any different, I believe, with regard to his individuality as a man. Here, again, it is a matter, in the first instance at least, of assimilating the tradition of humanity embodied in the institutions and records of the community in which he is brought up. Although this tradition is always open to correction, it is wrong to suggest, as Mill so frequently does, that the finer spirits of the community must be continually at odds with it on all points.[19]

Academic freedom is a part of our American tradition, and Mr. Commager, in defying tradition itself (except a curious tradition of denouncing tradition), threatens the freedom which gives him his opportunity to shout unto the world that he and his friends have no freedom of speech. Mr. Commager can dissent with impunity only while some of us still affirm with resolution. The Communists have very little use for Mr. Commager's dissention on principle. Protestantism, in the beginning, was strong and brave because it protested, not *against* tradition, but in favor of what it took to be true tradition: the word "protestant" meant a man who affirmed his principles strongly. The latter-day secular protestantism of Mr. Commager is all a negation, praising liberty because liberty gives opportunity to demolish ancient things, and praising the Academy because the Academy may be utilized as a safe corner from which to dislodge the wisdom of our ancestors. I am quite willing to fight to defend Mr. Commager's vagaries, but I object to fighting under his banner. Academic freedom has survived all these years through the vigilance of men who affirmed, not the ability of men who elevated their doubts into dogmas of negation. Dean Robert E. Fitch, writing in *Commentary*, says that Professor Commager talks of loyalty, "but is much more eloquent on what loyalty is not; and, even when he offers some rather specific answers to his question, makes all his values turn fuzzy at the edges through his inordinate contempt for absolutes and his passion for non-conformity."[20] If the scholar exalts relativism, skepticism, and impressionism at the expense of true belief, Mr. Fitch continues, he has a choice of only two roles: first, that of court chaplain, to "provide a spiritual gloss" over the naked follies of the time; or, second, that of court jester, to make a mockery of all values. In neither of these roles will he receive, or deserve, the freedom of the Academy. He will be a servant, in short, no matter how much Mr. Commager and Mr. Taylor and Mr. Hutchins talk of his independence.

If academic freedom is to be preserved through this dark time, the work must be done by men of a conservative bent. The principal tool of the conservative, in practical affairs, is prudence. In the following section, then, I shall try to suggest how, by some application of prudence, we may reconcile our principle of academic freedom with the necessity for expelling from the Academy men who have made themselves unworthy of that special freedom.

3

I enter now into the tangled thickets of loyalty-oaths, legislative investigations, non-juring professors, and all that labyrinth of suspicion and recrimination which has plagued our colleges these several years. This not being a history of academic freedom, but only an exploratory essay, I shall not endeavor to trace the course of the debate on such matters; I am trying merely to find a principle of order that may help to restore the dignity of the Academy. And I may as well declare at once the general view I take. In this, as in much else, my views are very close to those of the late Robert Taft. I think that the problems of subversion and indoctrination in the Academy must be solved by the Academy itself; I hesitate to recommend any sweeping proscription, even of Communists; and I believe that professors and legislators alike should speak and act with dignity, endeavoring with mutual respect to preserve the real freedom of the Academy.

First, let me set down my premises as to the relationship that ought to exist between the State and the Academy. In ordinary circumstances, the State (by which I mean any political organ of society) should abstain on principle from taking any direct part in the guidance or governance of our institutions of learning; and the Academy, taken as a body, should abstain on principle from a preoccupation with politics. Of course I do not mean that professors have no right, as private persons, to take a part in politics; of course they have. But I am saying that the Academy ought not to become an instrument for "training in democracy", or "inculcating liberal social views", or "preserving individualism". If it does any of these things deliberately, it must expect the State to interfere with its affairs, for it will have presumed to direct the State. Once the Academy undertakes indoctrination in an ideology, the State must and will regulate that indoctrination. Politics ought to be freely discussed within the Academy; yet the Academy ought not to try to exert direct influence in favor of some particular scheme of politics. Here lies one of the great dangers in the specious program for higher education in the Report of the President's Commission. If a principal aim—perhaps the principal aim—of higher education is to train citizens to conform to a particular ideology, and if the central government is to pay for this program, then the Academy becomes a mere propaganda-apparatus, and the professor becomes a clerk in the ministry of propaganda. Such clerks never are allowed independence of opinion.

In general, then, I think that State and Academy should live in separate houses. Only in grave emergencies is the State justified in taking a hand in the Academy's affairs. Our national government (despite the eagerness which the authors of *Higher Education in a Democracy* display to have the whole educational program in the United States guided by central authority) has no constitutional power to govern the policies of any of our universities, colleges, or schools; it did not found them, or grant them their charters, nor does it sustain them. The state governments, for their part, have little more authority over private colleges and schools; and where state-supported institutions are concerned, the part of prudence is to allow them to be regulated by the autonomous boards established for that purpose (ordinarily in the state constitutions), rather than by the executive and legislative branches.

Under what circumstances, then, are committees of Congress or of the state legislatures justly and prudently interested in the affairs of the Academy? Only if it appears that activities inimical to the security of the State are being carried on within the Academy (in which case, the State may protect itself as it would protect itself against subversion from any other quarter), or if it appears that the principles and structure of the Academy are in such a decayed state that the general welfare of society is imminently threatened. The investigations carried on by the several Senate and House committees into educational affairs generally are concerned with the first problem; and, considered abstractly, such an investigation is not improper. It may very easily be imprudent, of course. And I think that the State ought to conduct investigations of this sort only in extraordinary times, and then with the greatest respect for the dignity of the Academy.

I am not of the number of those scholars who denounce unrestrainedly the presumption of Congressmen and state legislators in daring to inquire into the integrity and sound judgment of professors. There is no reason to suppose that the average professor is a better judge of what affects the security of the United States than is the average legislator. It is undoubtedly true that Comunists have been at work in our educational

institutions, and that they might do much mischief there.*
Professor Zechariah Chafee, Jr., suggests that we ought to forget all about the world Communistic movement, and think
only of Communists in our colleges as "a small disaffected
minority group . . . with ideas considerably at odds with the
rest of us, but no more so than anti-Semites and ex-admirers
of Mussolini."[21] The trouble with this is that the Communists
do not think the same way; they are not concerned merely
with expressing erratic opinions unlikely ever to come to
fruition. They act as agents of a vast and remorseless power
that exerts absolute authority over many more people than
the millions that make up the population of the United States.
It is certainly true that Communist professors in this country
are not going to succeed in overthrowing our society by ex-
horting their students to man the barricades tomorrow; nor
are they such fools as to think so. The menace they constitute,
rather, is that of espionage and subtle, long-continued indoctrination. It is possible for them to betray certain secrets to the
Soviets, particularly in the physical sciences, and to some extent in the biological sciences. It is also possible for them to
conduct a long-range program of undermining the faith of the
rising generation in traditional society, and to form cells of
students who may be employed, in future years, to spread
Communist doctrines far afield. We can no more look upon
the American Communists as mere disagreeable eccentrics,
in these times, than the English state could afford to look upon
Jacobin organizations as mere clubs of impractical specula-

* Professor Charles I. Sillin thinks the folly of legislative investigations is proved by the fact that the House Committee on Un-American
Activities estimated that, at the height of their influence, the Communists in college and university faculties in this country numbered only
1500. But I do not think this is a negligible number; the Communists in
Russian universities were far fewer on the eve of the Russian Revolution.
As organizers of cells and mentors of fellow-travellers, Party members
can exert an influence out of all proportion to their numbers. (Charles
I. Sillin, "The Clear and Present Danger," *American Association of University Professors Bulletin,* winter, 1953-54, 595.)

tors, when the French Revolutionary fervor was at its height just across the Channel. If there were no Russia, these people might be harmless enough; but there *is* a Russia. Just how dangerous the Communists in our colleges have become is a matter for debate; but legislative bodies are neither tyrannical nor hysterical in looking into the matter. I think that the climate of opinion already has told heavily against the American Communists, so that not many members of the rising generation will be converted to that ideology; yet this does not mean that the Communists are no present problem; there is every reason why our constituted political authorities should exercise some surveillance over them.

I think, then, that the State does have a right to inquire into the extent to which a Communist conspiracy, or any other conspiracy, may exist in the Academy. The State has a right to protect its own security; and if the State is not secure, neither is the Academy. But as a practical matter, the efficacy of most legislative investigations is dubious. National and state legislators already are dismayingly burdened with a host of responsibilities, growing yearly greater as the scope of government is expanded in our time; and ordinarily they simply do not have time to conduct such investigations thoroughly and prudently. President Harry D. Gideonse observes that if everyone interested in this subject were to read the summary report of the Jenner Committee (July 17, 1953), *Subversive Influence in the Educational Process,* much of the acrimony which this controversy has provoked would seem pointless: "It would be clear that the committee is concerned with unprofessional conduct as it would be defined by any respectable academic authority. It would also be clear that the ordinary academic methods of inquiry are utterly inappropriate for the determination of the evidence that is relevant to the definition of conspiracy and of perjury."[22] The college, as Mr. Gideonse goes on to show, is not at present equipped to conduct such inquiries as legislative committees hope to accomplish. Neither, I am afraid, is the legislative committee itself; its work ordinarily is hasty and random. Both State and Academy need to develop more judicious and efficient techniques for looking into the possibility of subversion. Some persons have suggested that the United States ought to develop a new sort of investigatory agency, grave and impartial, on the model of the Royal Commissions of the British state. I do not propose to criticize that possibility here; I only venture to suggest that the structure of American government makes the creation of such bodies difficult. But until both State and Academy improve their methods of investigating subversion and indoctrination, we ought to be prepared to do what we can to assist such endeavors, when they are undertaken in a spirit of sincerity, with dignity and good will. As Dr. Gideonse suggests, it would be well to think about forming a national office, perhaps under the direction of the American Council on Education, with powers of subpoena and of citation for contempt, which could relieve legislative committees of this burden and be free of the imputation of personal or partisan motives. Meanwhile, we ought not to indulge in vehement denunciations of legislative committees which, after all, are the lawful agencies of democratic government. As Mr. Gideonse puts it:

> Rhetoric about the enduring values of free inquiry and attitudes of injured dignity will hardly suffice when congressional investigations reveal valid evidence concerning professional conduct that is demonstrably unworthy of a free profession. Under these circumstances, academic freedom is not preserved or enlarged by inaction. Only a strong and resilient response to the abuse *by the profession itself* will help to clarify and to strengthen the basic values of a free society and a free profession to which we are all dedicated.

The scholar and the teacher, whenever they are asked to take some part in a legislative investigation, ought to feel that, after all, the State is paying some respect to the influence of the Academy by this attention, not that they are so many mod-

ern Roger Williamses heroically defying a frowning orthodoxy. They ought to make the presumption that the politicians (as Mr. T. V. Smith suggests) are their friends, not their
enemies. I know that some legislators have behaved dis-
courteously and improperly; I know also that some professors
have treated legislators with contempt and arrogance. In general, we tend to be taken at our own valuation; and if learned
men behave with dignity and moderation, it is probable that
even the demagogue may learn civility from them. I am unable to understand how certain professors who are doctrinaire
equalitarians at the same time deny the right of a democratic
government to make even the most limited inquiry of them.
To take all from the state, and give nothing, results in the dissolution of society. On the other hand, I cannot agree that the
professor's views are public property in every respect; I think
that some people who ought to know better go too far in asserting that the teacher and the scholar "owe the public candor".
The matter of inquiry should be limited and well-defined; the
professor ought not to be expected to undergo a catechism on
every subject under the sun, whenever some popular passion
is aroused. I entertain hopes that both legislators and teachers
may come to entertain a higher respect for one another in
future.

Dr. Henry M. Wriston, president of Brown University, a
man not disposed to yield up the prerogatives of the Academy
to irresponsible political influences, states the general principle here succinctly:

> It is possible to argue (though not with much conviction since
> the courts have spoken) that *no one* should be asked, "Are you
> now or have you ever been a Communist?" But, if it is proper, as
> the courts say it is, to ask that question, it is fantastic to assert
> that professors should be exempt from responding. So long as the
> question is not outlawed, there is no basis for any claim to a
> "class" exemption. The question, the answer, and the compulsion
> involved have none of them anything whatever to do with
> "academic freedom."[23]

Too many professors have endeavored to guide themselves by what Professor Robert E. Cushman calls "principles of homemade constitutional law" when they have anything to do with legislative investigations, refusing to answer questions of any sort. Professor Cushman demonstrates that most of these people simply do not understand the federal and state laws on the subject, and, rather than sustaining our tradition of liberties, they go so far as to defy and abuse the rights of citizens: "I find myself wholly unable to agree that their well-intentioned obstinacy serves any useful purpose or advances any sound principle. I believe, on the contrary, that such conduct weakens the position of our colleges and universities by casting doubt upon the willingness of university teachers to assume the clear obligations of citizenship in a democratic state."[24] A professor who pleads his rights under the Fifth Amendment to our federal constitution ought to be aware that this protection against self-incrimination is intended as a concession to persons involved in criminal trials, against whom there is some presumption of personal guilt. It is not intended to enable citizens to treat constituted authority with silent contempt; and the man who invokes this protection must expect to produce a legitimate presumption in the minds of the authorities and of his colleagues that he has something to conceal that might subject him to prosecution. That the legislative committees and the courts have been lenient in dealing with professors who invoke the Fifth Amendment is no reason for teachers and scholars to abuse this prerogative. In plain fact, it is improbable that this defense could be persevered in, were legislative committees resolved to press the matter: it still is not a crime to be or to have been a member of the Communist Party, and no professor has been prosecuted for admitting that he was such. Merely that such an admission might cause him and his friends embarrassment, or even the loss of his position, is not a valid ground in law for pleading the possibility of self-incrimination. Society looks with justified suspicion upon anyone who, being asked legitimate questions by a lawful authority, retreats to this redoubt. I do not mean that universities ought invariably to discharge such a person; that is a matter for their own determination, to vary with particular circumstances; but to take advantage of the privileges of presumptive criminals is no vindication of academic dignity and no prop to academic freedom.[25]

The topic of loyalty-oaths is closely related to that of legislative investigations. Loyalty is the product of love; therefore it cannot be forced. A loyalty-oath, by definition, is a voluntary pledge. No one ought to be forced, therefore, to take such an oath, for his pledge, under such circumstances, would mean nothing. He might in theory, indeed, be liable to prosecution for perjury if, having sworn, he was proved to have been disloyal; but in practice, I know of no case in which a man has been subject to a criminal prosecution in a court of law for having broken an oath to a university. There have been several cases of persons discharged by universities (without resort to state courts) for what amounted to forswearing their pledges; but ordinarily the university's charge against them was that they "had misrepresented the facts" when first employed, not that they had broken a solemn covenant. Most "loyalty oaths" nowadays are really not much more than affidavits of freedom from Communist affiliation.

Though I say that no one ought to be compelled to subscribe to a loyalty-oath, it does not follow that no such test ought to be put to anyone. On the contrary, the administration of a dignified and properly-phrased oath to all persons at the time they join the staff of a university or college is entirely proper. There are some things that a teacher ought to be loyal to; if he cannot agree wholeheartedly to maintain that loyalty, then he ought not to take the oath, and he ought not to become a teacher at an institution which requires the oath. Nevertheless, if such an oath has *not* been administered when the teacher took up his duties, ordinarily it is unjust to require such a pledge long after he has settled down into his vocation. If the oath prescribes specifications which were not required when he commenced in his position, it tends to violate his rights of tenure; and sometimes, also, it may seem insulting to expect a teacher of long and honorable record to affirm that he will do in future what he had done in the past without any hesitancy.

Oath-taking is anything but the mark of servility. The president of the United States is required to take a solemn oath; the king of England is required to take a solemn oath. On the contrary, the requirement of oath-taking usually is a mark of mastery, a token that a man has come into his estate, and henceforth will occupy a place of trust and dignity. A man ought to feel honored, in most circumstances, that his fellows ask him to take an oath; for usually it immediately precedes the bestowal of high trusts and high duties. That there has been increased emphasis, the past few years, upon oath-taking in the Academy is in at least one respect a heartening symptom: it means that the public more and more regards education as a serious affair, and teachers as Bearers of the Word. I do not see why any teacher should feel humiliated at being requested to promise loyalty—provided that it is loyalty to true things that is expected, and that the pledge is asked in a spirit of respect, not in a spirit of contumely.

This said, let me add that I understand perfectly well the resentment evinced by many scholars and teachers who, in the past five or six years, have unexpectedly been required to swear to follow principles which they never had disobeyed, and that often in an undignified manner, unworthy of true oath-taking, in response to political pressures of the moment. The most celebrated case of this sort is that at the University of California in 1950. A professor with personal experience of that controversy writes to me, "I lived through the period of storm and stress in the University of California at the time of the loyalty oath difficulties. It was an extremely confused and

149

confusing issue and, as I look back on it, I think the Regents, administration, and faculty were at fault in about equal degrees. Certainly, I heard utterances from fellow-members of the faculty that made me despair, at times, of the faculty's ability to state correctly the cause of academic freedom."

The Regents of the University had endeavored to require all teachers there to subscribe to a formal pledge of loyalty. The reason was dread of subversive activity—not merely that of Communists, but of collectivists generally. As originally suggested (June, 1949), the oath was moderate, and probably no abstract objection could be raised to it (at a state institution) except that it was purely political in character, and that it might have involved in difficulties some persons with tenure of their positions: "I do not believe in and am not a member of, nor do I support any party or organization that believes in, advocates or teaches the overthrow of the United States Government by any illegal, unconstitutional means." What *was* objectionable, however, this oath was to be imposed upon teachers and scholars who had been allowed no hand in its framing; it was less suitable and dignified than an oath already required of every newly appointed member of the faculty;* as matters developed, it was to be required that teachers subscribe to it annually, a meaningless and humiliating repetition; and the Regents were impatient of any opposition. The consequence of all this was a rebellion on the part of the professors and a long and fierce controversy, in the course of which some 194 members of the staff were dismissed—although eventually the courts ordered their reinstatement. Changing ground presently, the Regents proposed to substitute for the proposed oath a similar statement inserted in annual contracts which each member of the staff must sign to

---

* "I do solemnly swear (or affirm) that I will support the Constitution of the United States and the Constitution of the State of California, and that I will faithfully discharge the duties of my office, according to the best of my ability." This is simply the standard oath prescribed for public offices and trusts by the Californian constitution.

obtain his salary; but this, in effect, would have abrogated the rights of tenure, and so only made the quarrel the more heated. The grounds on which the faculty opposed the idea of a loyalty oath were extremely varied. Some opposed all oaths; others protested against ill-treatment of Communists; others declared that this was only the first move in a scheme designed to drive all liberals out of the university; others objected to various phrases in the oath; yet others were angered not so much by the oath itself as by the general attitude of the Regents. In the long run, the professors won.

To my mind, the best remarks on this affair are contained in a pamphlet written by a professor of history at the University, Mr. Ernst H. Kantorowicz. He opposed the oath because of the heated atmosphere in which the proposal was brought forward; the reduction of the freedom of the faculty at which it hinted; the suspicion and contempt of professors which seemed to lie beneath it; the fact that it was repetitious and therefore contrary to the spirit of true oaths, which are permanently binding and sacred; the certainty that, in its altered form, it was designed to abolish the rights of tenure; and— this most important of all, perhaps—because the Regents were acting on the assumption that university teaching was not a high profession, with its prescriptive rights, but merely a trade, to be governed only by the usual terms of simple commercial contracts. His words on this last point are well worth quoting: "The Regents' efforts to make teaching a trade is entirely revolutionary. Should they succeed, their inconsiderate experiment would violently transform one of the few remaining conservative institutions, the University, and it would uproot one of the few relatively conservative sectors of modern society, that of university professors."[26]

Despite the unfortunate tone sometimes taken by certain professors who opposed this oath at California, and despite the confused arguments they sometimes put forward, the defeat of the Regents' policy, by court action, was a victory for true academic freedom, in the sense that Mr. Kantorowicz expresses it. The particular oath proposed was ill-framed, and probably superfluous; and no oath which awakens the resentment of a great part of a university's faculty ought to be insisted upon. Mr. Kantorowicz's discussion, founded upon conservative principles, suggests what an oath ought to be, if professors are to take an oath.

I think, first of all, that any such oath should not be purely political in character; for that implies that political opinion is the only thing to be got in a university which is worth taking seriously; and, at best, it implies that though professors may be trusted in other matters, they cannot be trusted in politics. Second, I suggest that any such oath employ only general terms so far as political fealty is concerned: a simple declaration that one will support the constitution, or the republic, is much better than a negative rejection of Communist affiliation. Third, I think that such an oath should be administered solemnly and formally, only once, and that when a teacher begins his work at an institution. Fourth, I recommend that provision be made to exempt, in appropriate degree, persons who cannot take such an oath without the possibility of infringing upon some previous oath—citizens of foreign nations teaching in the United States, for instance.

To frame such an oath positively will not be a simple matter. Some oaths that have been proposed at universities would be tyrannical impositions upon many members of the faculty; only a few years ago, for example, it was seriously proposed at Ohio State University that all professors be required to take an oath by the terms of which they would promise to teach only by the "empirical method"—that is, the system of John Dewey. Expostulation and threats of resignation defeated this suggestion. With the decay of commonly-acknowledged objectives and methods in education, it is now more difficult than ever before to draw up a pledge of loyalty that would offend no man's conscience, and I shall not attempt it with any precision here. Perhaps I may be allowed, nevertheless, to suggest that it might include a promise to adhere to the Truth, according to the light that is given to the teacher; a promise to conserve the wisdom of our ancestors and to extend the empire of knowledge as best a teacher can; a promise to guide and awaken the student, but not to indoctrinate; a promise to abide by the principles of social order, as expressed in the country's constitution; and a promise always to put freedom of the mind above material advantage and the passions of the hour. What the Hippocratic oath is to the physician, such an oath ought to be to the teacher, and more; and no further oath ought to be required by any authority.

This oath should be the voice of a conscience speaking to a conscience; for, as Professor Kantorowicz makes clear, what distinguishes the high profession of the Academy from an ordinary trade is the peculiar conscience of the scholar:

> From whatever angle one may look at the academic profession, it is always, in addition to passion and love, the conscience which makes the scholar a scholar. And it is through the fact that his whole being depends on his conscience that he manifests his connection with the legal profession as well as with the clergy from which, in the high Middle Ages, the academic profession descended and the scholar borrowed his gown. Unlike the employee, the professor dedicates, in the way of research, even most of his private life to the body corporate of the University of which he is the integral part. His impetus is his conscience. Therefore, if you demoralize that scholarly conscience, that love and passion for research and for teaching, and replace all that in a business fashion by strictly defined working hours, prescribed by the "employer", you have ruined, together with the academic profession, also the University.[27]

In fine, I think that only an oath which recognizes the peculiar character and mission of the Academy is worth taking, and that it should be administered, and taken, in a spirit of dedication, not of suspicion.

Last, in this chapter, I must say something about the problem of dealing with totalitarians in the Academy—at present, with Communists. Or perhaps I should not say "totalitarians", but rather "enemies of order"—any persons who would violently tear up the roots of society, regardless of tradition and prudence, for the sake of some fancied terrestrial paradise, or else simply out of detestation of harmony and things established. The only such fanaticism which seriously affects the Academy just now is Communism; at another time, or in other countries, it might be necessary to deal similarly with anarchism, or Nazism, or syndicalism, or some other fierce ideology which exalts force over reason and political abstraction over the peace of the civil social existence.

Should ideologists of a violent and conspiratorial affiliation be allowed to remain in the Academy, which is dedicated to reason and toleration? Practically speaking, have Communists a right to teach? This question, gradually coming to a head as even leftward-verging liberals in America became aware of the dread nature of the Soviet power, seems now to have reached climax at the University of Washington, in 1949. Until then, perhaps the majority of American professors, although increasingly uneasy about Communists in America, still would have been inclined to say that a Communist might teach. A committee of the legislature of the state of Washington undertook an investigation of purported communist activities at the state university, in July, 1948. At its hearings, ten members of the faculty were named as being or having been members of the Communist Party. Charges were brought by the University against six of these; and, after hearings, three of the six were discharged from the University, on February 1, 1949. The grounds upon which the dismissal was based, by the president and the regents, was that membership in the Communist Party in itself disqualifies a scholar for the high responsibilities to truth that are a professor's. "Having established the nature and characteristics of the Party as inimical

154

to the future welfare of the institutions of freedom in the United States," President Allen wrote, "it follows that secret membership in such a party . . . disqualifies them for membership in the faculty of the University of Washington within the causes for dismissal listed in the Administrative Code—specifically on the grounds of incompetency, dishonesty, and neglect of duty."[28]

The decision was hotly debated throughout the United States, and has not ceased to be discussed since; but by this time the bulk of opinion on the subject favors the attitude taken by President Allen. Liberal professors, among them Mr. Sidney Hook and Mr. T. V. Smith, maintained that the dismissal was justified; they have carried the day, in effect; and now I do not know of one college president in the country who states that he would knowingly engage a Communist, and surely there are very few who would retain one upon a college faculty. Harvard University has announced officially that no Communist will be allowed to retain a post there; and Harvard is as bold as any university in the United States. It was predicted at the time of the University of Washington case that a wave of persecution against "liberals" of every hue would follow; but as Professor Hook maintains, nothing of the sort has occurred. Mr. David Riesman remarks, "In our time, professors may have become conformists in many respects—there may be fewer 'characters' among us—but I am struck with how many, provided they are anti-Communist, have held on to Marxist views without being vilified or pressured."[29]

The arguments of those scholars who think the Washington decision unjust are sufficiently expressed by Professor Howard Mumford Jones:

What is really alleged by administrators is not that the offending instructor is romantically a conspirator against the peace and dignity of the United States; what is usually now said is that, by virtue of being a member of the Communist Party, the offending instructor has a closed mind and is therefore no longer fit to teach.

This is very attractive doctrine. It carries considerable weight and immensely simplifies the administrative problem. It gives the administrator a great moral advantage, and takes every advantage, both moral and intellectual, away from the man who is fired. He has no possible retort. If you are classified as belonging to a category of citizens whose minds are closed, it is clear that you do not belong in the academic community, where minds are supposed to be open. But I strongly infer from my experience and observation, after a lifetime of teaching, that the first criterion of an open mind is not to make absolute statements about men. . . .

Moreover, it is not merely the known Communist (if you can discover him) who is to be denied appointment because he has a closed mind; it is the potential Communist who is not going to be hired—that is, anybody upon whom somebody else can, as we say, hang something.[30]

This is the doctrinaire liberal speaking. The position of the scholars who believe that Communists cannot be tolerated because that toleration would be toleration of conspiracy and indoctrination is expressed clearly by President Raymond B. Allen of the University of Washington, in his concluding remarks upon the expulsion of the three professors from the faculty there:

Freedom is essential to sound education. That academic freedom must be maintained in any university worthy of the name is beyond question. But academic freedom consists of something more than merely an absence of restraints placed upon the teacher by the institution that employs him. It demands as well an absence of restraints placed upon the teacher by his political affiliations, by dogmas that may stand in the way of a free search for truth, or by rigid adherence to a "party line" that sacrifices dignity, honor, and integrity to the accomplishment of political ends. Men, and especially the teacher and the scholar, must be free to think and discover and believe, else there will be no new thought, no discovery, and no progress. But these freedoms are barren if their fruits are to be hidden away and denied. Men must be free, of course, but they must also be free, and willing, to stand up and profess what they believe so that all may hear. This is an important, if not the most important part of our American heritage of freedom. It is this American heritage of freedom that must be cherished and sustained by our systems and institutions of education if they are to survive.[31]

The national officers of the American Association of University Professors have endeavored, in some sense, to take a stand midway between these positions. Very briefly stated, they agree that the authorities of a college or university should not knowingly engage a Communist instructor; but that if a Communist is already established in the faculty, he should be discharged only if his conduct as a teacher and his ability as a scholar are so low as to warrant his dismissal on the same grounds as any other professor. Conspiracy, indoctrination, and fanatic inflexibility of mind are such grounds, of course, as the statements of policy of the AAUP make clear. Now Professor Hook is hard on the officers and leading members of the Association for this stand. As he suggests, there is no reason to suppose that a Communist long on the staff of a college is less dangerous than a newcomer; on the contrary, there is good reason to suppose that he is the more baneful for being the more experienced and hardened. Nevertheless, I am not altogether out of sympathy with the attitude of the AAUP.

For I believe, as did Senator Taft, that the decision to expel or to retain Communists on the staff of an educational institution should be made by the institutional authorities, and not by political authority; that conceivably some Communists may be competent professors who neither conspire nor indoctrinate; and that the decision as to whether they should be tolerated or dismissed must be made by the proper authorities in each case, without recourse to an invariable rule. I think, however, that membership in the Communist Party, or unmistakable fellow-travelling, is the most valid possible ground for a legitimate presumption that such a teacher will conspire and indoctrinate, and so is not qualified to teach. We ought not to forget, all the same, that just as some people professedly

Christian are not practicing Christians, so at least some few persons professedly Communist are not practicing Communists. I think that university authorities are justified in discharging a professor simply on the ground that he has been proved a Communist—either a Party member or a close collaborator; for, as Professor Hook says, it is nearly impossible to prove beyond all doubt that such a person actually has been conspiring or indoctrinating; students and colleagues are not informers. Nevertheless, trustees and president and faculty committees ought to be allowed some discretion in the matter; and if they decide that a professor, despite being a Communist, is no discredit to the Academy, then they ought to be allowed to retain him.

Actual membership in the Party ought not to be the only ground for dismissal for subversion: many of the persons most useful to the Communists have abstained deliberately from joining the Party—or may, in some instances, have been instructed to leave it opportunely. Where reasonable proof may be adduced that a fellow-traveller is not simply a sentimental trailer-in-the-wake of the Marxists, but an actual collaborator, as active in indoctrination as the Party member, such a person ought also to be dismissed. There, however—unless the college in question is a private or denominational institution and places definite restrictions, stated at the beginning of an appointment, upon radicalism of various sorts, as such a foundation has a right to do—we should draw the toleration-line. Beyond that point, in state institutions and in private colleges which do not declare their attachment to any particular set of theological or political principles, we ought to tolerate a wide variety of opinion. So long as professors do not take violence for the means to reform of society, so long as they admit the possibility of rational discussion, so long as they do not deliberately indoctrinate their students with their own prejudices, so long as they do not engage in a conspiracy against the civil social order—and so long, of course, as they are competent scholars—we ought to tolerate the conservative and the liberal and even the radical. Our Academy would be a dull and unhealthy place if such variety did not exist. Change, after all, is the plan of nature for conserving the life of society; without some change, we perish. But change unchecked leads straight to death, also; without permanence, we perish. In the Academy, accordingly, both the conservative bent and the liberal bent should not only be tolerated, but encouraged. If there were no liberals, we should find it necessary to invent some; if there were no conservatives—but perish that thought.

I do not mean that I think only the opinions of Communists are mischievous. I agree with Dr. Lynn White, Jr., president of Mills College, when he warns us against the centralized and totalitarian democracy which, even in America, threatens to supplant the democracy of elevation, decentralized and restrained: "The experience of our race during the last forty years has been so tragic that I do not see how anyone reared in the American tradition can fail to repudiate not merely communism and fascism but likewise that gentler approach to totalitarianism, monistic democracy."[32] So far as our twentieth-century "liberals" have forsaken the principles of individual freedom and diversity which were theirs until the past few decades, and have gone lusting after the limitless state, I think that they, too, are dangerous. But they are men with whom we can reason; they are not conspirators; and the better men among them, at least, like the better men among the conservatives, are not indoctrinators. And I hope, and see some indications, that many of the liberals who were slipping toward a totalitarian concept of the equalitarian society may win their way back to a liberalism like that of Mr. Jacques Barzun, say—attached to federalism or pluralism and to dispersion of power and authority, opposed to "efficient" centralization and bureaucracy.

And what of gentlemen like Professor Crawley, with whom we commenced this chapter? Why, when a scholar, whatever his private views, is not an indoctrinator, and not a conspirator, and has the good opinion of his colleagues, I think we ought to do all in our power to protect him against the impulses of the hour and the crowd. I do not think that such people will be in much peril if they have the courage to speak frankly and to stand up for themselves. Not very long ago, in many colleges, it was a good deal less safe to be a conservative than to be a radical; the people in authority approved of "progressive views" and "social consciousness". An anonymous professor not long ago wrote in the *Saturday Evening Post* (September 30, 1950) that no hearts bleed for conservative teachers' rights:

> This raises the question as to whether we might not properly be concerned with the academic freedom of conservatives. . . . This is no idle question. I remember sitting in on an interview with a prospective teacher who was subtly informed by a liberal interviewer that applicants of New Deal persuasion would have a better chance. . . . On campuses dominated by fanatical doctrinaire liberals, conservatives whose scholarly labors led them to the "wrong" interpretations would be denied merited promotions or otherwise penalized. Until greater wisdom and tolerance prevail among our "liberal" teachers, university authorities may well hesitate to give them more power over their moderate colleagues. A purge of conservatives and moderates is easy to imagine on some campuses.

It is not quite so easy to imagine in 1955, perhaps, as it was in 1950; but I do not think that the Professor Crawleys, by and large, are notably insecure. Some, like Henry Mulcahy in *Groves of Academe*, may actually entrench themselves against discharge for any cause by the pretense that they are former Communists who must not be discriminated against—at least, this is still a possibility on certain "progressive" campuses. Such is the way of the world. We never are going to obtain perfection in toleration, or in any aspect of academic freedom; but we all, conservatives and liberals alike, need ever to remind ourselves that our little private stock of reason is often insufficient in petty things, and sometimes insufficient in great.

V

The Dignity of the Academy

TWO DECADES AGO, Professor Arthur O. Lovejoy, writing
in *The Encyclopedia of the Social Sciences*, expressed
his conviction that freedom of opinion and expression
among professors was gaining ground, and that we might expect a continued growth of the rights and dignity of scholars
and teachers. Events have not borne him out. Probably there
is a greater degree of toleration at some denominational colleges, particularly in religious opinion, than formerly; certainly no one is discharged nowadays because he squints toward
bimetallism; and the growth of the Association of University
Professors has put some check upon arbitrary administrators
and trustees. But whether the mind of the average professor is
really more lively, and whether his actions are bolder, I doubt
profoundly. A gentleman who has done much to defend academic freedom writes to me that, with a great many people,
academic freedom means simply the right of a professor to
insulate himself from ideas. The yearning after "security", so
marked a characteristic of nearly every order of society in our
time, has tended to counterbalance the opportunities for vigorous thinking and teaching which the leaders of liberalism in
the colleges expected to arise out of the dissolution of old
prejudices.

"Sometimes I wonder," the liberal college president says in

The Groves of Academe, "whether we're on the right track, whether as creative persons we shouldn't live with more daring. Can you have creative teaching side by side with this preoccupation for security, with the principle of regular promotion and recognition of seniority? God knows, in the big universities, this system has fostered a great many academic barnacles." Surely anyone familiar with the American university must be struck, now and then, by the realization that a great many professors do not want freedom, really, for themselves, and certainly not for others: they are interested in fatter salaries, security of tenure, and the right to doze. They are aroused about "freedom" only when there appears to be some risk that their monopoly of indoctrinating students with their own prejudices may be impaired; they have no respect for the student's freedom of mind, nor for that of such irritating colleagues as may differ with them. Though they may go through the motions of "research", they care precious little about the duty to extend the boundaries of knowledge, and not very much about the duty to conserve the knowledge of our civilization. The humiliating pressure which many administrators endeavor to exert upon teachers to *publish*—to publish just anything, anywhere, for the sake of the record— or to draw up enormous committee-reports about trivialities suggests that both administrators and teachers are ignorant of the true nature of academic freedom and academic dignity. All the administrator wants is some tangible evidence of busy-work to present to his trustees or to the state legislature; all the teacher wants is some sham-proof of his liveliness of mind that may bring him a two-hundred-dollar increase in salary. How much freedom do such men have? And how much do they deserve?*

---

* I am told of a new dean who assembled the faculty before him and declared, "Now, you men have been teaching here all these years, and I'm sure you've done a good job of it. You must have had something to say. The time has come for you to *write it down*. Write it down, and

To want to extend the boundaries of knowledge, or to conserve the wisdom of ancestors, some faith in the importance of learning, and in a Good that is more than private gain, is required. That lacking, the teacher becomes a hired hand, paid to do a chore; and, naturally enough, soon he is treated as a servant. Even while they whisper and sigh about threats to academic freedom, such teachers are surrendering without one qualm of conscience the high functions with which academic freedom is inseparably joined. The automobile-worker on the assembly line enjoys no special freedom; he has no duties which require a special freedom. And if the teacher willingly assists in the reduction of formal education to a mere degree-mill intended to keep young people very mildly occupied, as if they were in an inordinately expensive kindergarten, then he surely will lose his academic freedom.

Whatever constriction of academic freedom may have come to pass in recent years because of timidity about expressing political opinions, this loss is very small in comparison with the diminution of true freedom of the intellect through a deadening but voluntary conformity to pragmatic smugness and the popular shibboleths of the day. Canon Bernard Iddings Bell describes this mood in *Crowd Culture,* and Mr. Alan Valentine in *The Age of Conformity.* Repeating the slogans of educational demagogues as if they were so many magical incantations, teachers who have yielded to this unwitting servitude call any suggestion that our system of education might be improved "fanatical", and any defense of true individuality and personality "undemocratic". The very people who are most voluble in their protests against alleged political conformity may be most indifferent to the decay of real intel-

---

publish it!" Of the making of books, truly there is no end; but there may certainly be an end to the patience of readers. A conspicuous fault of the higher learning in America is not a paucity of writing by professors, but rather a superfluity of it—a dismaying abundance of pedantic, valueless, and inarticulate writing.

lectual energy, or may even defend that latter tendency. Professor Commager, for instance, informs us that we need have no fears about American education because "more young people are going to college today than went to high school only thirty years ago." It does not appear to have occurred to his mind that conceivably this may mean merely that our colleges have been converted into high schools, and our high schools into socialization-factories. The schools, he continues, "provided a citizenry as enlightened as any on earth. They justified and vindicated democracy's promise."[1] With Mr. Commager, at least, one may hope to appeal from Philip drunk with doctrine to Philip sober with history, and recall some rather different observations he made two years earlier, in his *American Mind;* then he doubted if the American mind was more mature in the twentieth century than it had been in the nineteenth or the eighteenth: "Americans had experimented with mass education on a scale never heretofore attempted and its college and university population was as large as that of the rest of the world combined, but it was not certain that Americans as a whole were either better informed or more intelligent than their nineteenth century forebears; neither the level of the press nor the standards of literature had improved noticeably, while the popular culture represented by the lyceum or the Chatauqua of earlier generations was more sophisticated than that represented by the radio."

No such appeal, however, is possible where the people who run the National Education Association are concerned. When one reads their utterances at their convention in New York in 1954, he is apt to be reminded of Burke's observation that "men of intemperate minds cannot be free; their passions form their fetters." These gentlemen cried out that the nation is being frightened into a "sterile education", teachers not daring to touch upon the topics of Communism, sex, socialized medicine, and Lord knows what. Something rather ludicrous spoiled the effect of these remonstrances; for no one is quicker to crush any opposition, where theories of pedagogy are in question, than these very educationists; indeed, they spent much of their time at the convention doing just that. What the educationists seemed to desire was that all teachers should be free to conform to the dogmas of the National Education Association. The number of persons genuinely desirous of freedom of thought and expression, in our society, I repeat, is dangerously small.

The true hunger for independence of mind, and the true devotion to traditional learning, without which academic freedom is an organized hypocrisy, seem to me to be feeble among us. This feebleness appears to be part of a general atrophy of purpose, what C. E. M. Joad called "dropping the object". It has been observed by Mr. David Riesman, who inquires, "Why . . . are Americans often so anxious and unhappy, when Europeans, who live much closer to military or economic disaster, are so sanguine in their personal lives, often expressing philosophies of despair with exuberant arrogance? Why are American young people so frequently aimless, lacking private passions and pursuits, when a greater variety of skilled careers is open to them than ever before? Why in intellectual circles is there so much malice, when there are jobs and prestige and tasks enough for everybody and to spare?"[2] I do not propose to suggest any adequate answers to these questions here; but I do suggest that much of the whimpering one hears with respect to the subject of academic freedom, as contrasted with the vigorous assertion of the duties of the Academy, is part and parcel of the social boredom upon which Mr. Riesman touches. Again, then, I say that academic freedom is really desired only by a few men, and that a considerable part of the modern clerisy has neither true desire for it nor true right to it. It is the more important, therefore, that we set to work building whatever defenses we may about the idea and the institution of academic freedom, in a time when the sincere disciples of Socrates are very few.

First I shall suggest the improvement of certain institutional or constitutional defenses of academic freedom; then, in the second and third sections of this chapter, I shall have something to say about the reformation which must occur in our educational system, and the reformation which must occur in the character of our scholars and teachers, if academic freedom is to remain more than a god-term. I think that we ought to pay some attention to the following aspects of the educational structure which gives form to academic freedom.

(1) We ought to encourage the development of university or collegiate senates, made up of the faculty, wherever such bodies do not now exist; and we ought to respect the powers of such bodies where they exist already. Free discussion of the great problems in education—not merely political questions, but all the principal topics upon which men's opinions differ—is a better guarantee of responsible performance of duties within the Academy than any amount of exhortation to "serve the people" or to "teach democracy". These faculty senates ought to have a considerable part in determining the chief policies of the institution; they ought not to be mere advisory bodies. I do not mean that our colleges ought to be turned into soviets of teachers. The founders and benefactors and alumni of a university have a right to exert a reasonable supervision over general policies, and the president needs to have power enough to restrain the senate from carrying on a perpetual debate that would prevent any action. But such a senate is a mark that professors are not considered mere hired hands; that the subtleties of higher education must be undertaken by learned men; and that most important matters in the Academy are not intended to be entrusted solely to administrative functionaries, while the scholar and the teacher are left to arrange the trifling details.

(2) We ought to make sure that the men who administer the affairs of our universities and colleges, the executives, are scholars first, and administrators second—even if this (and I

doubt it) means a loss of efficiency. In the past fifteen years, particularly at our state institutions, there has been a most ominous tendency to elevate to authority men who are fond of authority for its own sake (a dangerous policy anywhere, and especially in the Academy), and men who are "good business-men" (and ought, therefore, to be in business, not in the Academy), and men who are trained in pure "education" without knowing anything about any particular branch of learning, or having any clear concept of a liberal education in general. Mr. Henry Allen Moe puts this difficulty clearly:

> In the big academic worlds men who enjoy the kind of work called administration normally become chairmen or directors or other administrators. Such men recognize and are drawn to their kind, with whom they are at ease, and thus, year by year, the selection of men for university posts tends to proceed in this direction. This is not the result of design, but is mainly a direction of congeniality of temperament that, consciously or unconsciously, wishes too much the result that is commonly called cooperation. But you see what the process does: it tends gradually to eliminate the significant variants, the persons who are interested in unfamiliar ideas, those who lack a definitive label, those whose interest and bent cannot be named by a word, those lonely seekers whose intellectual curiosity and creative imagination come to flower and fruition only when left alone, uncooperatively except as they themselves seek out kindred souls.[3]

Thus the intellectual leadership which a college president, or any other principal administrator, ought to exert slips away; a barrier is formed between the administrators and the professors; the domination of a body of learned men by a corps of administrative technicians is a standing insult to the Academy, and a standing threat to academic freedom. In an extreme case, it ends in the conduct of someone like President Stout toward someone like Professor Richardson. I have no easy remedy for the tendency toward educational bureaucracy. But I think that once the danger is acknowledged, we have come some distance toward guarding against it. I am inclined to believe that our administrators ought to be conscript fathers, in effect, as they usually are at the British universities: scholars who are compelled or induced to assume administrative responsibilities, rather than experts in public-relations and accounting who seek just such positions.

(3) We ought to try to ensure that our boards of trustees or regents are composed of men of liberal learning and large views. Some private foundations, and even some state institutions, are so fortunate as to have such boards already; but many do not. It ought to be recognized that boards of trustees have responsibilities that are not purely financial and that, therefore, financial talents are not the only qualification necessary for elevation to such a board. I do not say that businessmen ought not to serve; indeed, I am sure that many of them ought to serve; but it will be well to emphasize that they are chosen not merely because they are practical men of commerce and industry, but because they are that and something more. Nomination to the governing boards of state institutions ought not to be by popular vote; the general public cannot possibly know the qualifications of candidates for such an office. They might be nominated by the governor of the state, as is now proposed in Nevada, or nominated by a responsible body of alumni, or by a combination of these two methods. And most of them ought to come from the educated professions and the scholarly disciplines.

(4) We ought to allow the alumni of American colleges and universities a respectable place in the governance of their institutions. I agree with Mr. Buckley that the alumni have a right to be heard; but I think that to throw all authority into their hands at once would be catastrophic. Even at Harvard, alumni associations, as now constituted, sometimes have been more baneful than beneficent. Football and reunions at present are almost the sole concern of alumni groups, and nearly every college encourages them in this preoccupation; most

administrators seem to feel that the alumni naturally will have ceased to read books or to take any interest in the works of the mind, once they are free of compulsory attendance at classes, and so should be utilized merely as ticket-hawkers during the football season. I think that we ought to experiment with the possibility of making each graduate a permanent member of the General Council of the university, as at the Scottish universities, with a right to be heard at the annual or biennial meetings of such a council. Only a comparative few would take any active part in such gatherings, but those few might reason intelligently, and all alumni might acquire some sense of responsibility. If the affairs of the institution seemed to be going very badly indeed, such a council might undertake measures of redress.

(5) We ought to do everything in our power to save our private universities and colleges from financial ruin, toward which most of them are rapidly sliding. The firm stand of Harvard University against political dictation reminded some equalitarian liberals that academic freedom is most secure in our better private foundations, and must always be so, because of their independence of financial policies of political bodies, and of direct political interference. Our private institutions remain, moreover, as so many Megaras in which our Platos and Euclids can take refuge from the democratic despotism of Athens. This whole subject would require a volume to itself for adequate discussion. I throw out here, nevertheless, the suggestion that we might divert a part of the money which states and municipalities are lavishing upon education into the treasuries of private institutions, without ringing in political supervision, if we were to set up systems of state or municipal scholarships for deserving students, the students to go to whatever institution they might choose. Thus we could avoid the extravagantly expensive foundation of new state universities and colleges (of the sort at present being undertaken by New York and Massachusetts) and insure the

survival of our private foundations that have done so much to form the American character. It is by this method that the British state makes higher education available to everyone fit to profit by it, and yet remains clear of political mastery over the universities.

(6) We ought to do something about professors' salaries: it is an insult to learning that the teacher and the scholar, at the highest levels of education, should be rewarded no better than the barber, and not so well as the bricklayer. (Often enough, indeed, public-school teachers in our larger cities receive higher pay than distinguished scholars at universities.) Either we ought to increase salaries, or we ought to diminish them. If the learned man is to be rewarded financially at all, even in the sense of an honorarium, he ought to be rewarded more generously than the mechanic; and I think that our country is rich enough to do this. A man whose remuneration is determined in the commercial market, and there determined to be approximately that of a journeyman carpenter, is not going to hold any very high opinion of his status in society, nor to stand by the duties and prerogatives which appertain to his order; nor will the mass of men regard him with any higher respect.

If, however, our society will not resolve to increase professors' salaries, then our society ought to diminish them. In that event, the American professor would be like the professor at the University of Vienna today—bitterly impoverished, shabby, almost a mendicant; but in Vienna, everyone expects him to be just that, and admires and honors him for it, and treats him with a respect accorded to no one else. For in Vienna it is clear that the professor does not work for wages, or even for an honorarium, but simply because he is a dedicated man, who loves learning more than food, and thinks that to conserve and to seek the truth is its own reward. This attitude already is what makes it possible for most Catholic universities and colleges to survive in America, of course: their endowment is the unpaid priests and nuns upon their faculties. If we reduce salaries, we certainly will cleanse the Academy of everyone but the dedicated man, who will not be afraid to defend his freedom because he has next to nothing to lose, and whom no administrators or trustees will try to intimidate, because they could find no one to replace him. The real income of the average factory-hand has increased by 160 per cent, in this country, since 1908; the real income of the average professor has not increased at all—at many respectable colleges, indeed, it has fallen since 1908.[4] You may pay the honorable man a decent honorarium, or you may not pay him at all; but it is difficult to secure the loyalty of any honorable man by paying him plain wages, as if he were a hired hand, and then paying him badly.

How the professor's salary may be increased is a topic too elaborate for thorough discussion here. Yet I will say that much could be accomplished, at more than a few institutions, simply by prudent retrenchment, the savings to be applied to the increasing of the salaries of true professors of arts and sciences. Infatuated by magnitude, the majority of our institutions have tried either to undertake a multitude of tasks not strictly educational, for which they do not have money enough, or else have invited in a crowd of students for whom they cannot employ enough teachers at decent salaries. Some are going to have to make this retrenchment soon, or else cease to exist. It is also true that at our larger universities, and especially at our state institutions, we often pay salaries to all sorts of people who are not professors at all, really, but simply technicians of one sort or another, with no claim to academic freedom and its prerogatives. We may pay an instructor in "airline stewardess training" more than a professor of botany, or a "professor" of boys'-camp management more than a professor of history. It is interesting and irritating to compare the salaries of professors of education, at most universities, with the salaries of professors of arts and sciences. In short, if we really want to treat our scholars and teachers as dignified human beings, we are going to have to begin to discriminate.

Let me add here that I have found those persons with some private income to be the most ready defenders of academic freedom, generally. Their hostages to fortune are in the background, not forever reminding them that they are utterly dependent upon a college's bounty; and though they may not be always conscious, in their resolution, of their total or partial independence of administrators' dislikes, nevertheless they act habitually with greater confidence. A college which has a number of such persons on its staff is fortunate. I suggest to doctrinaire levellers that here, as in much else, the reduction of private means by taxation or inflation is a very serious blow to freedom of action.

So much for practical suggestions toward the protection of our academic freedom. I know that the problem cannot be intelligently discussed in terms of institutional devices alone. I proceed now to venture some remarks upon the faults of educational principle and professorial character which must be recognized if we are to make headway against the blind forces inimical to all our learning and liberty.

2

Professor Ernst Kantorowicz declares that the most alarming aspect of the California loyalty-oath controversy was the Regents' attitude that a professor is a servant, employed at a trade, and not a learned man who is invested with the dignity of a high profession. But this doctrine was repudiated, or at least contested, at the University of California; while at some of our institutions, particularly the state technological and teachers' colleges, the professor is regularly treated as an "employee", and he seldom protests—indeed, he is treated as an inferior sort of employee, less essential than bookkeepers and typists, and is ordered about with an arrogance that the college administrators never would dare manifest toward any laborer who happened to be a member of a trade-union.

There are colleges where the first act required of a new professor-employee is that he strip himself naked, to be prodded by a college doctor, as if he were being hired for service in the mines of the Rand; if he does not submit to this promptly, an official notice informs him, he will not be paid his salary that first month. The salary is kept always in the foreground; the professor-employee never is allowed to forget that he is bought with a price. Before he is permitted to teach his first class that term, he is converted into a clerk at student-registration, and a vast horde of bewildered freshmen descends upon him, their hands and pockets full of business-machine cards, and they vaccinated and photographed and herded like so many criminals, all at the double; the other professor-employees snarl at them, and the more experienced students treat the professor-employees with contempt. When the college gets down to the disagreeable business of teaching, the new professor-employee finds himself confronting a roomful of motley boys and girls, nearly all of them very badly schooled, and a considerable portion of them positively averse to learning anything: these came simply for college fun, or social snobbery, or on athletic scholarships, or because they expect to make a great deal of money out of a degree in a few years. Sometimes the majority of the class do not read—not even the textbook; they expect knowledge to be poured into them, like milk into a bottle, and do not hesitate to reproach the professor-employee if he departs from Holy Writ—that is, the textbook; they think that lectures are designed for the recital of that sacred text, to save students the bother of reading it. Often enough (and especially if this is a freshman or sophomore course) the professor-employee is ordered to teach a prescribed topic in a prescribed way on a prescribed day; and the principal examinations, made up by other people, consist of multiple-choice questions which can be scored by the business-machines. The scope of the course may be so impossibly vast, and the time allotted for study so very short, that it is hopeless to expect any intelligent discussion of any matter; besides, the students are kept busy every night by the seven-ring circus that plays perpetually at the college, socializing them—dances, club-meetings, travelogues, ice-skating, football rallies, and all the rest. Under the circumstances, the professor-employee cannot hope to persuade his students to read or to think; he can only indoctrinate them in certain approved generalizations. If he is given a cure of graduate students, the authorities expect him to see that these promising young people get their theses written and approved, even if (as very often happens) he has to write them himself. At best, he is permitted to fail one or two students in a class; and the administration smiles upon him if he fails none at all; this latter proves that he must be a very good teacher; and no administrator wants the enrollment decreased by arbitrary standards of scholarship. Is not growth, sheer growth, the object of all life? What does a college exist for but to grow, like the industrial concerns it models itself upon? Students are encouraged to come to the head of the department, and the dean, and report their opinions of the professor-employee. Is he "over the head" of the average student? Is he unsympathetic? Doesn't he amuse a class? Does he stick, as he should, strictly to the syllabus? If he fails to satisfy his students in such particulars, the authorities will reprove him. After all, the professor-employee is there to serve the students, to make them feel at home. He doesn't want to be out of a job, does he?

The girl-clerks in the administration building treat the professor-employee to a steady diet of hauteur when he ventures in, cap in hand, to sign the forms for his compulsory life-insurance and his optional hospitalization-plan. Naturally: he must be a poor creature to spend his time teaching boys and girls, when he might be in the insurance-business himself. One of the more affable janitors may condescend to say "Good morning, Prof," to him, occasionally: the janitor can afford to condescend, for he is paid more than the professor-employee, like enough. The dean calls him into his office when trouble is in the wind: he doesn't want to be bothered with an unprosperous professor-employee otherwise. If the professor-employee is satisfactorily submissive, he may even be allowed to teach through the summer months, for several hundreds of dollars extra in wages. If any of this seems a trifle disagreeable to the hired hand—why, he is informed very promptly that no one at this institution is indispensable.

Now of course I have been describing one of the less mannerly of our enormous overcrowded campuses. The trouble is that these places are growing in size and number, and that an increasing proportion of what the nation spends upon higher education is allotted to just these places. The wave of the future seems to be surging their way; "service to the public" and "education for democracy" are their slogans. At least one-fourth of our small private colleges will be extinguished within five years, we are told; but not one of these Behemoths will give up the ghost.

Nearly half a century ago, Irving Babbitt, foreseeing this chaotic mass-production "educational institution" of the future, suggested at the end of his *Literature and the American College* the true mission of the college in American democracy:

Our colleges and universities could render no greater service than to oppose to the worship of energy and the frantic eagerness for action an atmosphere of leisure and reflection. It would seem that they might recognize the claims of the contemplative life without encouraging a cloistered seclusion or falling into the monastic abuses of the past. We should make large allowance in our lives for the "eventual element of calm," if they are not to degenerate into the furious and feverish pursuit of mechanical efficiency. The industrial democracy of which President Eliot speaks will need to temper its joy in work with the joy in leisure, if it is to be a democracy in which a civilized person

175

would care to live. The tendency of an industrial democracy that took joy in work alone would be to live in a perpetual devil's sabbath of whirling machinery, and call it progress. Progress, thus understood, will prove only a way of retrograding toward barbarism. . . . The present situation especially is not one that will be saved—if it is to be saved at all—by what we have called humanitarian hustling. We have already quoted the federal judge who exhorts the American people to combine ten per cent of thought with ninety per cent of action. If we ourselves ventured on an exhortation to the American people, it would rather be that of Demosthenes to the Athenians: "In God's name, I beg of you to think." Of action we shall have plenty in any case; but it is only by a more humane reflection that we can escape the penalties sure to be exacted from any country that tries to dispense in its national life with the principle of leisure.[5]

No room is left for leisure in the "educational institution" I have described, nor for true thought; the professor-employee is there to indoctrinate his cure of students in approved attitudes; and then they will go out to make money and run their machines. But just now I am concerned principally with what hope there may be for academic freedom in such an atmosphere.

I think that very little hope for academic freedom lingers in such circumstances. In what respect are the scholar and the teacher free? At the very best, they may aspire to be allowed to hold private political opinions; and if they happen to hold the right sort of opinions, usually of a vaguely liberal and humanitarian character, they may be allowed to preach them to their students. But they cannot be free to seek the truth, for neither college nor students, on such a campus, can afford to take time for that indulgence; and they cannot be free to conserve the wisdom of our ancestors, for everything is to be taught "in relation to present needs"; and they cannot be free to assert the primacy of contemplation over all the forms of action, for that would be insolent heresy at an institution of this character. They are hired to do a job, very truly, and that job is to get boys and girls through the degree-mill as expeditiously as possible, and with as few qualms of conscience. After all, the public pays them, and pays them more than some old-fangled private college would, in all probability. Just what sort of academic freedom do these professor-employees expect? And just what sort do they deserve? What sacred trust are they guarding? Just how much do they themselves care about Truth? Some of them have on their shelves no books but a few free copies of textbooks; some of them talk, when they meet together, only of salaries and faculty scandals; some of them say that this state of affairs is a positive good, and look forward with relish to the demise of private foundations which, with intellectual snobbery, still cling to standards.

Yet I do not despair utterly of some reform even at these monstrous institutions; nor do I think academic freedom may safely be ignored even there. No debatable land exists between the liberal intellect and the servile intellect: if professors and students reside in an atmosphere of "democratic" servility and conformity to the idols of the marketplace, presently that climate of opinion will spread heavily over the face of the nation. It will not suffice for freedom of thought and expression that academic freedom be allowed, on sufferance, to persist at a few small colleges, or here and there at some old university, while the mass of students are indoctrinated in an amorphous materialism and the mass of teachers are bullied into renouncing the hopes of accomplishment and duty pursued which many of them entertained at the beginning of their career. I think that we shall have to address ourselves to the titanic difficulty of restoring personality, meaning, and freedom to these inchoate campuses, where students sleep three in a room in their dormitories, and television blinks and blares at either end of their study-lounges, and the juke-boxes in the Union insure that no one ever shall escape from the sense of "togetherness". If these institutions were simply technological institutes, or even simply schools of pedagogy, it might be said that the question of academic freedom would not be much affected by such places, since they would have very little share in those studies in the liberal arts and in pure science which traditionally have been associated with academic freedom. But nearly all of these colleges have ceased to confine themselves to their original purposes, and now teach, or try to teach, nearly every branch of learning, and enroll a multitude of students in "core courses" intended to supplant the liberal arts curriculum; indeed, they set up their own graduate-schools and confer doctoral degrees with as great an enthusiasm as any of the older "Ph.D. factories" at some Middlewestern state universities. In some degree, the faults which these institutions display so conspicuously are the faults, too, of most state universities and of many private colleges that have grown enamored of aggrandizement. And, compelled to compete for government appropriations or for students with these colleges of the new type, the older institutions tend more and more to lower their standards of instruction, and their sense of the dignity of the teaching profession, proportionately. That dignity and academic freedom are inseparable: if the professor is not allowed to retain any shred of dignity, he will not long retain any rag of freedom. The restoration of academic freedom, then, must be undertaken without further delay at precisely those colleges where academic freedom always has been feeble. To bring back some dignity to these institutions, it will be necessary to give the teachers some respect for themselves; to teach the students some respect for their calling and for learning itself; and to remind the college administrators that they are not really industrialists, but members of the clerisy. All this makes a hard row to hoe.

The teacher cannot respect himself if he feels that he is the prisoner of a mob of "students" who do not study, who want only to doze or to be amused, and who cannot be introduced to the freedom of ideas because they have no foundation of facts upon which the professor may establish, with their co-

operation, some premises. What most colleges are doing nowadays is simply what inferior high-schools were doing thirty
years ago: that is, to try to cram a little knowledge of history,
of economics, of politics, of literature, of physical science, of
biology, of mathematics, of simple grammar and orthography
and composition, into the heads of young people. Their previous schooling has consisted almost entirely of "co-operative"
projects" and "learning by doing" and "fun with numbers" and
vague round-table discussions of World Problems and Good
Neighborliness; they cannot write a coherent paragraph, and
they cannot support the sociological generalizations in which
they have been encouraged to indulge by any historical or
geographical evidence, and they have no mastery of any simple discipline of art or science. Ironically enough, some of
the best high-school graduates remaining—they make their
mark in college—are those who attended "technical" high
schools, originally vocational in purpose, where mathematics
and other disciplines have not yet given way entirely to a
debased "progressivism". Confronted by this abyss of ignorance, the most that the average college-teacher can hope for,
in the run-of-the-mill college, is to impart a little factual
knowledge to these young people, so that they may make a
beginning toward liberal education; but by the time most
of them have got anywhere, they are ready to graduate; and
the professor, in the process, has been compelled to forget
his early hopes of discussing general ideas and beauty and
truth and the ends of scholarship with his students. He is very
fortunate, indeed, if he has escaped the hostility of many of
the students and the reprimands of the administrators in the
course of his attempt to impart even simple facts; for the student got in high-school the notion that his role in education
was to express himself, not to learn thoroughly; and the administrator really is concerned, in a large number of colleges,
with maintaining a prosperous custodial institution, not with
the difficult task of helping people to think.

Faced with these obstacles, it is a remarkable professor who can retain full self-respect, and true love of learning. Some sink into apathy; others go along with the tide, and cease to teach, spending their class-hours in quips and quizzes; yet others leave the profession in disgust. And this condition is not going to be remedied—remedied nowhere, not even at the University of Chicago or Harvard University—until the primary and secondary schooling of the young people who enter college is reformed. What those reforms ought to be, a number of abler critics than I have suggested in recent years. They must include a training in the simple disciplines by which knowledge is acquired and the mind prepared to reason logically—grammar, spelling, mathematics, written composition, a fundamental acquaintance with great literature, history, geography, biology, physics, and similar subjects without which any curriculum becomes a mere confused congeries of "socialization" projects and random skills. They must include some discipline of character and manners, inculcating a decent attitude toward scholars and scholarship. They must include a realization that knowledge is not something to be poured into students by servant-teachers, but an infinitely valuable property to be got only through severe personal striving. I know that immense difficulties obstruct the reform of public-school education upon any such pattern. I also know that until something of the sort is accomplished, the teacher will think less and less of himself, in our colleges, and his academic freedom will decline together with his academic dignity.

Such a reform of elementary and secondary schooling must be accompanied by a reform of the college itself. Probably it is vain to expect any contraction of the present swollen state of our institutions of higher learning, which is calculated to annihilate the quiet and the atmosphere of contemplation that are the chief traditional advantages of college study: trustees, and administrators, and the professors themselves, have acquired such a stake in maintaining enrollments at their present level that the advocates of retrenchment are in a lean and proscribed minority. But what we can attempt is to improve the quality of our present institutions, instead of expanding insensately, and to seek to distinguish between the Academy and mere custodial institutions, so that some genuine universities and colleges may remain worthy of their name. As things are going, we will have nothing but custodial institutions left in this country. We might do well to establish, in any institutions of higher education that still want to educate, two programs of study and two categories of students; we might call the first an "honors" program, in which students who really want to think and to read will be encouraged to enroll, and for which a distinct degree will be conferred; while the rest of the college, and the rest of the students, may be allowed to play at the Hollywood-image of college life. This will be expensive, but probably not so costly as an indiscriminate expansion of our campuses with no ends in view but producing a general mediocrity of intellect, and gratifying snobbery by enrollment at college without the intention of improving mind or character. Just now, we are vaguely trying to make our graduate schools do what the college used to do; but the graduate schools are ill adapted, by their structure, to the task. In our anxiety to give everyone a college degree, we are giving no one an education. A professor who declines to the estate of a mere scoutmaster or club chaperone is not going to be allowed any considerable degree of academic freedom, because everyone, before long, will know that he is a whited sepulchre.

Other people are writing books about these difficulties and their remedy. I am only saying here that a man who sincerely believes in academic freedom, if he is consistent, must believe in some discipline, discrimination, and purpose in higher education. The scholar and the teacher are invested with a peculiar liberty to speculate and talk about values only because they are supposed to believe that values exist. The sort of professor-servant likely to succeed under the regime of "mass education", in the present chaotic sense of that phrase, is the man who knows the price of everything and the value of nothing.

3

Not long ago I was present at a conference of scholars held in one of our great endowed libraries.* Nearly every person participating was a professor of some reputation; most of them had published books or articles that established their claim to authority in some traditional field of knowledge; many of them had years of teaching at well-known universities to their credit. The discussion came to center round the aims of a university education. I am not much given to illusions about our professors, and yet I was startled at the attitude which most of these people, explicitly or implicitly, were not in the least abashed to manifest. For the majority of these gentlemen held that university education has *no* aims; like Topsy, an American university just grows; it exists "to satisfy a demand"; if it satisfies that demand, the appetite of the market-

* I hope that these noble and munificent libraries, like the Huntington, the Newberry, and the Folger, gradually may assume some of the functions which the university used to undertake, at least until some of our universities reform themselves. It is not fantastic to speculate upon the possibility of installing the Academy, driven out of our nominal educational institutions, in these foundations—so many little All Souls' Colleges. Too little attention has been paid to the truly humane education which might be obtained at such places by readers with scholarships and finished scholars who could combine research and contemplation with the discourse among learned men that makes the Academy into something more than an Educational Plant. Mr. Hutchins, in *The Conflict in Education,* seems almost ready to give up our universities as damaged beyond repair by empiricism, specialism, and positivism; and he suggests that "we may require another institution, which would leave the university to go on as it is doing now, which would not supplant the university, but which would take up the burden the university has laid down." It would make possible "a continuous Socratic dialogue on the basic issues of human life."

place, it expands and prospers; if it opposes that demand, it fails. Now there happened to be present at this gathering some men of finance and commerce, trustees of the great library; and I observed that these latter gentlemen were taken aback at hearing such opinions expressed by professors, the Bearers of the Word. The men of business still clung to an obdurate prejudice that a university stands for something: what it stands for may be in dispute, but at least it has *some* ends. The professors, being in the know, were disdainful of such oldfangled notions: *they* knew universities from the inside; they knew that what university presidents were after was aggrandizement, and that what professors were after was advancement. They took it for granted that they profited from a racket —not a very lucrative racket, perhaps, in comparison with some others, but nevertheless a Good Thing for those who were on the inside. They were willing enough to teach anything to anyone who might ask for it; and—though perhaps I am unjust to them in this—I suspect that they were willing enough to teach whatever side of a question the received opinion of the hour might seem inclined to reward. These were properly sophisticated scholars; they were, in plain fact, Sophists. One of the younger professors quoted with approval an utterance of the president of one of the sprawling state universities: "There is no program of study to which we will not stoop if the public seems to desire it."

I have said that the businessmen present were governed, in part, by prejudice, which (properly understood) is only another word for the wisdom of our ancestors; while the professors, or rather the dominant group among them, were governed by what they took to be pure reason and pragmatic sanctions. But there was also another difference sufficiently distinguishing the businessmen from the professors: the businessmen around that conference-table tended to think as free men think, *liberally;* and they rather liked it when the chairman of the meeting quoted Newman's definition of a univer-

sity as a place where the liberal understanding is to be cultivated. But the professors (I mean, again, the pragmatists
dominant among them) spoke in another language: they
talked of "service to the public" and "satisfying a demand"
and "adjusting to the industrial age". They spoke after the
habit of men who are accustomed to obey, rather than to
command; to conform, rather than to explore. They did not
even go out to battle, like the Celts of the Twilight, resigned
to defeat, yet resolved to keep what they might from the
wreck of worlds. No, they were perfectly willing to hew wood
and draw water for Demos, or Pragma, or Behemoth, or Mr.
Minister of Propaganda; they might talk manfully, on occasion, about threats to the freedom of the intellect—but, as
Dr. Johnson remarked of the butcher, "When he says his heart
bleeds for you, he means nothing by it." This, too, was simply
part of the patter of the trade. They thought and spoke, in
short, servilely. Master knows best. When someone spoke of
university education abroad, a number of these gentlemen
protested that they knew American education to be superior
to any system of higher learning in all the ages and all the
continents; and, secure in this confidence, they had not wasted
their time going abroad to confirm it. A slave is a being who
habitually submits to having his choices made for him by
some other man.

I am not implying that men of finance and commerce are
the best possible guardians of the Academy. They are not:
their calling does not fit them for this duty; when a business-
man is competent to be a patron of the Academy, for the most
part it is in spite of his calling, not because of it. The businessmen at this conference were successful and superior businessmen, it is true; but, then, the professors were successful
and superior professors. Yet if the businessmen present were
reasonably well qualified to defend the Academy in spite of
their calling, the professors present (with some honorable
exceptions) were remarkably unfit to champion academic

freedom, also in spite of their calling. They stood for submission to the wave of the future and conformity to the mass-mind; while being swept away by the flood (to borrow a metaphor from J. F. Stephen) they were more than willing to sing hallelujah to the river-god. Just what manner of men are such professors of arts and sciences?

Well, it is some comfort to reflect that the Academy always has had a number of these gentry under its trees. A perceptive professor of politics, Mr. Francis Graham Wilson, distinguishes two great types of intellectuals: the philosopher in the Greek sense, the lover of wisdom, who is convinced that the human soul has transcendental aims; and the sophist, who teaches success in life, and disdains standards. When men are arming, the defense of the Academy always falls to the lot of the philosophers: the sophists, by that time, have joined the enemy or fled away to Sybaris. And yet it is part of the duty of the philosopher to preserve freedom in the Academy even for the sophist. So it is even now: democracy finds its best defenders in the men who think there is something higher in the universe than pure democracy, and academic freedom its most able champions in men who believe in just authority. Let me quote from Professor Wilson's strong essay:

It may seem paradoxical, but the intellectual who accepts a transcendental order that is above all men can be more easily reconciled to democracy and the forces of public opinion than one who does not. Such a view stands in criticism of much of the current theory of democracy. For in the intellectually predominant view of the present, democracy is almost incompatible with any standards that philosophy and religion may propose. It is asserted by some that only a philosophy of pragmatism is compatible with democracy. In other words, democracy must be based on something like William James' radical empiricism, or the instrumentalism of John Dewey. Or, one might say that because no standard of human justice can be proved, the only standard is that which is approved by some majoritarian procedure.

If this proposition states the current situation, it must arise from some qualities within the individual itself; it must be a kind of existential statement of the tensions of his life. In a direct sense, the answer may be found in the attitude of the intellectual toward political power. Those who deny a transcendental realization must attain whatever objectives they have in mind in the organization of society, and this primarily through the force of the state. Thus, they are driven to seek power, or sometimes in futility to deride it. On the other hand, those who, like Boethius, seek the consolation of philosophy, may speak of the vanity of the world. The order of wisdom is both here and beyond, and knowledge can be its own reward and spiritual consolation. Such an intellectual's primary activities are teaching and writing, so that the *artes liberales* will become the proud possession of the coming generation. He is happiest when he is directing a school, the Lyceum or the Academy in Athens, or perhaps the cathedral schools that preceded the foundation of the Western universities. What he asks is freedom from the ruler, not freedom to direct the government.

One is driven, therefore, to the conclusion that the intellectual who rejects the higher order of human experience is existentially a seeker of power. The free commitment of his will may be to him a painful experience, but in the end he has tried to remake the world; that is, historically, he has sought to be the servant and the advisor of kings.[6]

In our age, the doctrinaire secularist and the doctrinaire equalitarian seek to be kings' servants: that is, they run after King Dinos and King Demos. Power over men's minds, and popularity with the masters of society, suit them much better than the lonely search for truth; but such power and such popularity must be bought with a price; and that price is servility to the ruling spirit of the hour. When, however, somehow the king declines to be flattered, and somehow the reformers' plans for directing society lead to catastrophe, and somehow power insists upon corrupting, then this sophist turns to deriding power, or to deriding all authority: we behold the phenomenon of the sour and carping professor, going to some pains to persuade his students that he is blasé in a town which calls it Blaze; convinced (like Humpty Dumpty) that people are listening at keyholes and peeping around corners to catch him in some act of Promethean defiance; declaring that there can be no Heaven, or he would be in glory, and that there can be no Hell, or his critics would burn like straw.

Dean Fitch, describing this present mood among the pragmatic intelligentsia of America, at once timorous and strident, suggests that in some considerable part it is the product of a bad conscience—a feeling, however secret, lurks in the heart of the "liberal" sophist that somehow he was flirting with something highly baneful when he toyed with Communism. This worm gnaws at his inner consciousness. As Mr. Fitch suggests, the best way to purge a bad conscience is through repentance and confession; but this Christian doctrine is distasteful to the doctrinaire liberal; therefore, often enough, he endeavors to stifle his misgivings with an intensified self-righteousness:

> One may acknowledge in secret that one has been in error, and one may have actually moved on to new ways that are clear and clean. But it is impossible publicly to confess to error, then or now, so the intelligentsia believe, rightly or wrongly. So they take another course: any criticism of one's conduct, any allegation of grave mistakes of judgment, is to be met with outraged cries about the violation of civil liberties and the attack on integrity of conscience. This shabby kind of performance we have surely witnessed more than once. It springs from a deep instinct of self-preservation within the breasts of the intelligentsia. For there is one sin to which the professionally intelligent person may not confess without losing caste, without shearing off his own self-respect and the respect due him from others—stupidity! ...
>
> The simple fact is that, when the intelligentsia are on the defensive due to an unacknowledged bad conscience, they tend to develop a party line. Any slightest departure from the line is deviationism, and is punished accordingly. While they denounce, quite properly, the fanatical negativism that anti-Communism

can become, they develop a fanatical negativism of their own directed against those who threaten their security. While they protest against indiscriminate character assassination on the part of others, they practice a sort of reverse smear of their own, branding as McCarthyism whatever varies from their approved doctrine. While they object to guilt by association, they exercise against those who show the least disposition toward internal criticism of the group the much more effective and intolerant device of guilt by *dis*association: he that is not with us 100 per cent is against us![7]

This is the present plight of the Academician without standards or recognized values, the courtier of Dinos and Demos, the sophist denied power and so converted to the detestation of all authority. This professed bravo of the Groves of Academe is himself the most intolerant of mortals. We owe no toleration, I repeat, to those who would not tolerate us; and if this species of intellectual were the only inhabitant of the Academy, then indeed we had might as well throw open the gates to the rabble rout of zealots who would supplant the doctrines of the Sophist by the doctrines of the Covenanter.

But the modern Sophists are not the only men who walk in the shade of the Academy. "Because half a dozen grasshoppers under a fern make the field ring with their importunate chink," Burke says, we ought not to imagine "that those who make the noise are the only inhabitants of the field; that, of course, they are many in number; or that, after all, they are other than the little, shrivelled, meagre, hopping, though loud and troublesome insects of the hour." I hesitate to carry Burke's analogy further by comparing the truer Academicians to the great cattle chewing the cud in the shadow of the oak; yet the real scholar and the real teacher, even nowadays, generally retain a placidity, a mildness of temper, and an abiding strength which contrast radically with the shrill noises of the twentieth-century Sophist. And the real scholar and the real teacher, men broadly tolerant because they have convictions from which to tolerate error, quietly dignified because they know themselves to be Bearers of the Word, still compose the majority in our Academy. We are doing our worst to change them: we are setting administrative tyrants over them, and immersing them in a deluge of unfeeling students; nevertheless, they continue to bear more than any man should be expected to endure. The high-minded professor of French literature, endeavoring to communicate the subtleties of Pascal to a class of impatient young people eager to be off in their convertibles; the old-fashioned professor of mathematics, convinced that Euclid alone has looked on beauty bare, doing what he can to lead the intellects of future time-study men to the contemplation of order; the austere professor of philosophy, teaching Augustine to a generation filled with the concupiscence of the heart—these, and a few others like them, would make the endurance of any number of insects of the hour worthwhile. These scholars and teachers are not yet few, however; they are to be found in every college and university, retiring, often truly humble, wise as simple learned men are wise, kindly and generous in a time of triumphant egoism, dedicated members of the clerisy. I would spare any number of academic Sodoms out of reverence for such men; and I think, moreover, that if we had any way of counting noses in the Academy, we should find men not much inferior to this pattern more numerous than the sophistical grasshoppers. If we were to open the gates of the Academy to the Covenanters, it is not merely the Sophists who would be extirpated: with much that is baneful or silly, more that is wise and good would be hewed in pieces.

I have been saying this: that it is for the sake of the Philosophers that the Academy enjoys its freedom, and it is only out of concern for the Philosophers that the Sophists are tolerated in their license. If the Academy is to preserve its liberties in the Iron Age, it must be defended by men loyal to transcendent values. But to what values, precisely? Some of the most voluble critics of pragmatism, empiricism, and positivism, of the whole relativistic cult that afflicts the modern intellect, seem curiously feeble advocates of abiding truth when they come down to a declaration of their own loyalties. Mr. Robert Hutchins, after some slashing attacks upon the Sophists, ends with the following creed for Academicians:

> The leading articles of the American faith are universal suffrage, universal education, independence of thought and action as the birthright of every individual, and reliance on reason as the principal means by which society is to be advanced. To the extent to which the American people have now forgotten or distorted these ideas, to that extent they have strayed from their own path. This was the path to Utopia.[8]

Well! Could not Professor Commager have written these sentences with equal fervor and equal imprecision? Is this the freedom of the human reason for which Socrates drank the hemlock, and for which the poet and the philosopher have starved in their garrets? Universal suffrage—a means to an end, at best, and sometimes a danger, kept within limits only by the Providential law that the number of fools in opposite factions usually is in balance; universal education—which so often prefers uniformity to attainment, and compulsion to volition; independence of thought and action—with what motive? reliance on reason to *advance society*—not to make the human person his own master. These things are good, or indifferent, or positive evils, according to how they are employed. They are not ends. They have no sanction but expediency. And the path to Utopia? There is no path to Utopia; there is no Utopia, here below. This is the Gnostic delusion. One of the principal functions of the Academy, where society is concerned, is to save a people from Utopian fancies. If ever we arrived in Utopia, we should detest the place; such is the nature of human yearning.

To what truths, then, ought the Academy to be dedicated? To the proposition that the end of education is the elevation of the reason of the human person, for the human person's own sake. To the proposition that the higher imagination is better than the sensate triumph. To the proposition that the fear of God, and not the mastery over man and nature, is the object of learning. To the proposition that quality is worth more than quantity. To the proposition that justice takes precedence over power. To the proposition that order is more lovable than egoism. To the proposition that to believe all things, if the choice must be made, is nobler than to doubt all things. To the proposition that honor outweighs success. To the proposition that tolerance is wiser than ideology. To the proposition, Socratic and Christian, that the unexamined life is not worth living. If the Academy holds by these propositions, not all the force of Caesar can break down its walls; but if the Academy is bent upon sneering at everything in heaven and earth, or upon reforming itself after the model of the market-place, not all the eloquence of the prophets can save it.

Notes

Notes

CHAPTER ONE

1. Sidney Hook, *Heresy, Yes—Conspiracy, No,* pp. 154–61.
2. Robert M. Hutchins, *The University of Utopia,* pp. 75–77.
3. *Ibid.,* pp. 77–78.
4. Tappan's views are summarized succinctly in Mr. Edwin Mc-Cellan's article "The Educational Ideas of Henry Philip Tappan", *Michigan History,* spring, 1954.
5. The stormy history of academic freedom in the United States is discussed in Mr. Robert P. Ludlum's "Academic Freedom and Tenure", *Antioch Review,* spring, 1950, and in Mr. Richard H. Shryock's "The Academic Profession in the United States", *American Association of University Professors Bulletin,* spring, 1952. Thomas Jefferson's inconsistencies are described in Mr. Gordon E. Baker's "Thomas Jefferson on Academic Freedom", *American Association of University Professors Bulletin,* autumn, 1953.
6. "Academic Freedom and Tenure: Report of Committee A for 1950", *Association of American University Professors Bulletin,* spring, 1951, p. 74.
7. *Ibid.,* p. 79; and the later tabulations in the reports for 1951, 1952, and 1953, contained in the *AAUP Bulletin,* numbers for spring, 1952, spring, 1953, and spring, 1954.
8. Quoted by Mr. Robert Ludlum, *op. cit.,* p. 19.
9. Hutchins, *The University of Utopia,* p. 87.
10. Norman Thomas, *The Test of Freedom,* p. 140.

CHAPTER TWO

1. Alexander Meiklejohn, "The Teaching of Intellectual Freedom", *American Association of University Professors Bulletin,* spring, 1952, pp. 5–6.
2. John Dewey, *A Common Faith,* p. 42.
3. Douglas Knight, "The Colleges and the Rejection of Intellect", *Association of American Colleges Bulletin,* May, 1954, p. 226.
4. F. A. Hayek, *The Counter-Revolution of Science: Studies on the Abuse of Reason,* pp. 101–102.

5. Etienne Gilson, *Dogmatism and Tolerance*, pp. 7–13.
6. Colin Clark, "The Twilight of Liberalism?", *Encounter*, August, 1954, p. 61.
7. Sidney Hook, *Heresy Yes—Conspiracy, No*, p. 220.
8. Sidney Hook, *Education for Modern Man*, p. 2.
9. John Henry Newman, *Discussions and Arguments*, p. 272.
10. *Education for Modern Man*, p. 119.
11. Albert Lynd, *Quackery in Education*, p. 200.
12. *Education for Modern Man*, p. 11.
13. G. H. Bantock, "John Dewey on Education", *Cambridge Journal*, June, 1952, pp. 538–39.
14. John Dewey, *Democracy in Education*, p. 143.
15. *Heresy, Yes—Conspiracy, No*, p. 233; *Education for Modern Man*, p. 55.
16. Knight, *op. cit.*, p. 223.

CHAPTER THREE

1. Robert M. Hutchins, "What Price Freedom?", *American Association of University Professors Bulletin*, summer, 1949, pp. 211–12.
2. Robert M. Hutchins, "Are Our Teachers Afraid to Teach?", *Look*, March 9, 1954, p. 28.
3. Leslie A. Fiedler, "McCarthy", *Encounter*, August, 1954, p. 13.
4. Hutchins, *The University of Utopia*, p. 89.
5. Hutchins, *op. cit.*, pp. 89 and 47–48.
6. Harry D. Gideonse, "On Re-Thinking Liberal Education", in *Strengthening Education at All Levels*, p. 41.
7. Ralph W. McDonald, "A Half Century of American Education—1900 to 1950", *Association of American Colleges Bulletin*, October, 1954, p. 351.
8. Jackson Martindell, "An Educational Forecast", *Association of American Colleges Bulletin*, October, 1954, pp. 366–70.
9. Knight, *op. cit.*, p. 223.

CHAPTER FOUR

1. Mary McCarthy, *The Groves of Academe*, p. 291.
2. Colin Clark, *op. cit.*, p. 59.
3. For a summary history of benefit of clergy, see William Holdsworth, *A History of English Law*, III, pp. 293–302.

4. Henry Steele Commager, *Freedom, Loyalty, Dissent*, p. 71.

5. William F. Buckley, Jr., *God and Man at Yale*, p. 190.

6. Hoxie N. Fairchild, *Religious Perspectives of College Teaching in English Literature*, p. 6.

7. Alexis de Tocqueville, *Democracy in America*, I, p. 262.

8. Hook, *Heresy, Yes—Conspiracy, No*, p. 137.

9. *Ibid.*, p. 253.

10. Harold Taylor, *On Education and Freedom*, p. 306.

11. T. V. Smith, "Academic Freedom Revisited", in *Vision and Action*, p. 24.

12. H. S. Commager, *op. cit.*, p. 87.

13. Hutchins, "Are Our Teachers Afraid to Teach?", *Look*, March 9, 1954, p. 28.

14. Hutchins, "The Freedom of the University", *American Association of University Professors Bulletin*, summer, 1951, p. 245.

15. Irving Kristol, "Ordeal by Mendacity", *The Twentieth Century*, October, 1952, p. 315 ff.

16. William J. Newman, "Propaganda and the American Intellectual", *The Twentieth Century*, January, 1953, p. 34.

17. Commager, *op. cit.*, p. 92.

18. *Ibid.*, p. 155.

19. R. P. Anschutz, *The Philosophy of J. S. Mill*, pp. 25–26.

20. Robert E. Fitch, "The Fears of the Intelligentsia", *Commentary*, October, 1954, pp. 331–33.

21. Zechariah Chafee, Jr., "Freedom and Fear", *American Association of University Professors Bulletin*, autumn, 1949, p. 431.

22. Harry D. Gideonse, "Are Congressional Investigations Helpful?", *The Educational Record*, April, 1954.

23. Henry M. Wriston, "Education on the Razor's Edge", *Southwest Review*, autumn, 1953, p. 308.

24. Robert E. Cushman, *Academic Freedom and Responsibility*, p. 8.

25. Francis W. Coker, "Academic Freedom and the Congressional Investigations: Free Speech and the Silent Professor", *The Journal of Politics*, August, 1954, pp. 491–508. This is a most thorough examination of the rights of investigating committees and their witnesses.

26. Ernst H. Kantorowicz, *The Fundamental Issue*, p. 19.

27. *Ibid.*, p. 21.

28. *Communism and Academic Freedom: the Record of the Tenure Cases at the University of Washington*, p. 108.

29. David Riesman, *Individualism Reconsidered*, p. 129.

30. Howard Mumford Jones, "How Much Academic Freedom?", *The Atlantic Monthly*, June, 1953, p. 39.

31. *Communism and Academic Freedom, op. cit.*, pp. 108–09.

32. Lynn White, Jr., "Democracy and Private Education", *The Pacific Spectator*, winter, 1953, p. 17.

CHAPTER FIVE

1. Henry Steele Commager, quoted in *Time*, August 30, 1954, p. 48.

2. David Riesman, *Individualism Reconsidered*, p. 136.

3. Henry Allen Moe, "The Power of Freedom", *American Association of University Professors Bulletin*, autumn, 1951, pp. 468–69.

4. See Clarence D. Long, "Professors' Salaries and the Inflation", *American Association of University Professors Bulletin*, winter, 1952–53, p. 577 ff.

5. Irving Babbitt, *Literature and the American College*, pp. 261–62.

6. Francis G. Wilson, "Public Opinion and the Intellectuals", *American Political Science Review*, June, 1954, p. 333.

7. Fitch, *op. cit.*, pp. 331–32.

8. Hutchins, *The University of Utopia*, p. 102.

Bibliography

Bibliography

I HAD THOUGHT of drawing up a reasonably complete bibliography on this subject; but that work is being done by persons better qualified to do it, and the volume of periodical-writing about academic freedom is growing so rapidly that such a list would have been out of date before this book could have come from the press. I list below, then, only such books and pamphlets as I have mentioned in my text or in notes, together with a few additional books which I found useful. Periodical articles are listed simply in my notes.

Anschutz, R. P. *The Philosophy of J. S. Mill.* Oxford: The Clarendon Press, 1953.

Babbitt, Irving. *Literature and the American College.* Boston and New York: Houghton Mifflin Company, 1908.

Bantock, G. H. *Freedom and Authority in Education.* Chicago: Henry Regnery Company, 1952.

Barth, Alan. *The Loyalty of Free Men.* New York: The Viking Press, 1951.

Bell, Bernard Iddings. *Crisis in Education.* New York: Whittlesey House, 1949.

Bell, Bernard Iddings. *Crowd Culture.* New York: Harper and Brothers, 1953.

Bestor, Arthur E. *Educational Wastelands.* Urbana: University of Illinois Press, 1953.

Buckley, William F., Jr. *God and Man at Yale.* Chicago: Henry Regnery Company, 1951.

Buckley, William F., Jr., and Bozell, Brent. *McCarthy and His Enemies.* Chicago: Henry Regnery Company, 1954.

Burnham, James. *The Web of Subversion.* New York: The John Day Company, 1954.

Chalmers, Gordon Keith. *The Republic and the Person.* Chicago: Henry Regnery Company, 1952.

Chamberlain, Lawrence H. *Loyalty and Legislative Action.* Ithaca: Cornell University Press, 1951.

Commager, Henry Steele. *Freedom, Loyalty, Dissent.* New York: Oxford University Press, 1954.

Communism and Academic Freedom: the Record of the Tenure Cases at the University of Washington. Seattle: University of Washington Press, 1949.

Conant, James Bryant. *Education and Liberty.* Cambridge, Massachusetts: Harvard University Press, 1953.

Countryman, Vern. *Un-American Activities in the State of Washington.* Ithaca: Cornell University Press, 1951.

Cushman, Robert E. *Academic Freedom and Responsibility.* Ithaca: Cornell University Press, 1952.

Dewey, John. *Democracy and Education.* New York: The Macmillan Company, 1916.

Dewey, John. *Reconstruction in Philosophy.* Boston: The Beacon Press, 1948.

Fairchild, Hoxie N. *Religious Perspectives of College Teaching in English Literature.* New Haven: The Edward W. Hazen Foundation, 1950.

Freedom and the University. Ithaca: Cornell University Press, 1950.

Gellhorn, Walter. *Security, Loyalty, and Science.* Ithaca: Cornell University Press, 1950.

Gideonse, Harry D. "On Re-Thinking Liberal Education", in *Strengthening Education at All Levels,* a Report of the Eighteenth Educational Conference, 1953, held under the Auspices of the Educational Records Bureau and American Council on Education. Washington: American Council on Education, 1953.

Gilson, Etienne. *Dogmatism and Tolerance.* New Brunswick, New Jersey: Rutgers University Press, 1952.

Griswold, A. Whitney. *Essays on Education.* New Haven: Yale University Press, 1954.

Grodzins, Morton. *Americans Betrayed.* Chicago: University of Chicago Press, 1949.

Hayek, F. A. *The Counter-Revolution of Science: Studies on the Abuse of Reason.* Glencoe, Illinois: The Free Press, 1952.

Hicks, Granville. *Where We Came Out.* New York: The Viking Press, 1954.

Higher Education for American Democracy: a Report of the President's Commission on Higher Education. New York: Harper and Brothers, 1948.

Hocking, William Ernest. *Experiment in Education: What We Can Learn from Teaching Germany.* Chicago: Henry Regnery Company, 1952.

Holdsworth, W. S. *A History of English Law*. 12 vols. London: Methuen and Company, 1908-52.

Hook, Sidney. *Education for Modern Man*. New York: The Dial Press, 1946.

Hook, Sidney. *Heresy, Yes—Conspiracy, No*. New York: The John Day Company, 1953.

Hullfish, H. Gordon (editor). *Educational Freedom in an Age of Anxiety*. New York: Harper and Brothers, 1953.

Hutchins, Robert M. *The Conflict in Education in a Democratic Society*. New York: Harper and Brothers, 1953.

Hutchins, Robert M. *Education for Freedom*. Baton Rouge: Louisiana State University Press, 1943.

Hutchins, Robert M. *No Friendly Voice*. Chicago: University of Chicago Press, 1936.

Hutchins, Robert M. *The University of Utopia*. Chicago: University of Chicago Press, 1953.

Kantorowicz, Ernst H. *The Fundamental Issue: Documents and Notes on the University of California Loyalty Oath*. Berkeley, California: privately printed, 1950.

Kirk, Russell. *St. Andrews*. London: B. T. Batsford, 1954.

Lynd, Albert. *Quackery in the Public Schools*. Boston: Little, Brown and Company, 1953.

Lewis, Wyndham. *Self Condemned*. Chicago: Henry Regnery Company, 1955.

McCarthy, Mary. *The Groves of Academe*. New York: Harcourt, Brace, and Company, 1952.

Moberly, Sir Walter. *The Crisis in the University*. London: SCM Press, 1949.

(National Association of Manufacturers). *This We Believe about Education:* a Statement concerning Education in America. New York: National Association of Manufacturers, 1954.

Newman, John Henry. *Discussions and Arguments on Various Subjects*. London: Longmans, 1873.

Newman, John Henry. *The Idea of a University Defined and Illustrated*. London: Pickering, 1875.

Oxnam, G. Bromley. *I Protest*. New York: Harper and Brothers, 1954.

Riesman, David. *Individualism Reconsidered*. Glencoe, Illinois: The Free Press, 1954.

Smith, Mortimer. *And Madly Teach*. Chicago: Henry Regnery Company, 1949.

Smith, Mortimer. *The Diminished Mind.* Chicago: Henry Regnery Company, 1954.

Smith, T. V. "Academic Freedom Revisited", in *Vision and Action.* New Brunswick, New Jersey: Rutgers University Press, 1953.

Stewart, George R. *The Year of the Oath.* New York: Doubleday and Company, 1950.

Taylor, Harold. *On Education and Freedom.* New York: Abelard-Schuman, 1954.

Thomas, Norman. *The Test of Freedom.* New York: W. W. Norton and Company, 1954.

Valentine, Alan. *The Age of Conformity.* Chicago: Henry Regnery Company, 1954.

Except for newspaper accounts, almost nothing has been published concerning the case of Mr. Couch at the University of Chicago and the case of Mr. Richardson at the University of Nevada; but I have been able to consult extensive files of documents and correspondence in either case.

Numerous articles on academic freedom have been published during the last five or six years in the critical and scholarly journals, particularly the *Bulletin* of the AAUP, the *Bulletin* of the Association of American Colleges, the *Antioch Review*, the *American Scholar*, and some of the quarterlies of political science.

Index

Index